IN HARMONY WITH NATURE

IN HARMONY WITH NATURE

▪▪▪▪▪▪▪▪▪ LESSONS FROM THE ▪▪▪▪▪▪▪▪▪

ARTS & CRAFTS GARDEN

TEXT AND PHOTOGRAPHY BY

RICK DARKE

FRIEDMAN/FAIRFAX
PUBLISHERS

Acknowledgments

A great many friends and acquaintances have casually enriched my understanding of the Arts & Crafts movement, its people, and its landscapes, and I wish to extend warm thanks to all. Many people and places contributed directly to the research, ideas, and materials that resulted in this book, and to them I owe a special note of appreciation: Chip Arena, Dianne Ayres, Mansfield Bascom, Ruth Esherick Bascom, Bill Benson, Mr. & Mrs. Simon Biddulph, the staff of Bok Tower Gardens and Pinewood House, Ted Bosley, Mr. & Mrs. Neil Bunis, the Carson Valley School, Prudence Churchill, Craftsman Farms, Descanso Gardens, Wharton Esherick Museum, the community of Essex Fells, Fallingwater, the Gamble House, Gravetye Manor, Great Dixter, Green Gables, Isabelle Greene, the Greene & Greene Library, David Hart, Hestercombe, Historical Society of Southern California (El Alisal), Mr. and Mrs. Edward Hollamby, Tim Hansen, Paula Healy, Hedgerow Theater, Russ Jones, Kentuck Knob, Vance Koehler, Philip Larson, Susan Lauzau, Phaedra and Mark Ledbetter, Rob Leonard, Little Thakeham, Christopher Lloyd, Malmesbury Cathedral, Beth Ann McPherson, Tommy McPherson, Louise Mills, Mohonk Mountain House, Moravian Pottery and Tileworks, Morris Arboretum, the community of Mountain Lake, Ruth Peck, Seth Peterson Cottage Conservancy, Mr. & Mrs. William F. Porter, E. Morris Potter, Tim and Pauline Ractliff, Colvin Randall, Michele Raymond, Cleota Reed, Penelope Reed, Stuart & Miriam Reisbord, the community of Rose Valley, Fred Ryan, Richard Schulhof, Jonathan Shaw, Mary Ann Smith, Bruce Smith, Fred Spicer, David Streatfield, James Swasey, Taliesin, Taliesin West, Judith Tankard, Mark Taylor, George Thomas, Mrs. & Mrs. Wirt L. Thompson Jr., Paul Van Meter, Rosemary Verey, Susan Waggoner, Willowwood Arboretum, Bob Winter, Winterthur Museum, Gardens and Library, Melinda Zoehrer.

PAGE 2: *Ferns and red valerian* (Centranthus ruber) *spill onto an entry walk at William Robinson's Gravetye Manor, while vines including* Parthenocissus *bring the garden to the upper reaches of the manor house.*

A FRIEDMAN/FAIRFAX BOOK

© 2000 by Michael Friedman Publishing Group, Inc.

Library of Congress Cataloging-in-Publication Data available upon request

10 9 8 7 6 5 4 3 2 1

EDITOR: Susan Lauzau
ART DIRECTOR: Jeff Batzli
DESIGN: Lindgren/Fuller Design
PHOTOGRAPHY EDITOR: Wendy Missan
PRODUCTION MANAGER: Richela Fabian
PHOTOGRAPHS: © Rick Darke

Color separations by Radstock Repro
Printed in England by Butler & Tanner Ltd.

For bulk purchases and special sales,
please contact:
Friedman/Fairfax Publishers
Attention: Sales Department
15 West 26th Street
New York, New York 10010
212/685-6610 fax 212/685-1307
Visit our website: www.metrobooks.com

Contents

Preface

Thinking about what gardening means to me, I imagine I am much like many readers of this book. I want my garden to be a place where I can express my own insights and creativity, and celebrate the innovations of my time as well as local traditions. It should be an inspiring place to share with friends. The garden must also reflect a reverence for the physical essence of my region and its larger living community, those things we often call Nature.

The turning of a century seems to inspire a time of great reflection and evaluation, especially when it coincides with a period of radical change in science, technology, and culture. We are living in such a time, as were the proponents of the original Arts and Crafts Movement. Then, as now, a great deal of debate was focused on the proper balance of nature and culture.

Though my training is in horticulture and the natural sciences, like many, I was first introduced to the Arts and Crafts Movement through its decorative objects. I eventually discovered that the Arts and Crafts ideals embodied in such objects were also beautifully expressed in the gardens of the period. The best of these gardens displayed a sophisticated vision of nature and culture, where man and nature exist not in opposition but in harmony. The beautiful diversity of nature was closely observed and seen as something worth emulating and preserving, yet there was also a firm belief that human endeavor could be a positive influence on nature. My subsequent

The landscape of Bok Tower Gardens is glimpsed through a panel in the tower's great brass door. Metalworker Samuel Yellin chose the image of a great native oak for this unique see-through panel.

studies have revealed a wealth of inspiration and ideas that hold great relevance for today's gardeners.

Though garden design ranks with the finest of arts, a garden is among the most ephemeral of art forms, and is typically outlived by fabrics, furniture, and ceramics. Fortunately, though many Arts and Crafts landscapes have been lost to time, a fair number have survived or been restored. My work has afforded me the opportunity to visit and photograph a great many Arts and Crafts gardens in Great Britain and across North America. I've been lucky to wake up in many of these gardens, to share meals and conversation in them. My journeys have left an indelible mark on my own understanding of the garden and how richly it can contribute to the character of daily life. This book is a distillation of these lessons learned from the Arts and Crafts garden.

Part One

BIRTH OF A MOVEMENT

The warm tones of a hand-hammered copper drawer pull adorning an L. & J. G. Stickley table reflect the low luster of the native woods.

LEFT: At Green Gables, an avenue of Camperdown elms speaks eloquently of Charles Greene's love of big trees, of light and shadow play.

ORIGINS

OPPOSITE: *Fruit trees remain an elemental part of the gardens at Great Dixter, providing both sustenance and a connection to earlier orchards.*

he twentieth century's astounding array of scientific and technological achievements has changed the look and feel of workplaces, homes, and common landscapes beyond our dreams and, in some cases, beyond desire. It is increasingly apparent that we must develop a sensitive vision of the future that allows us to celebrate the best of our innovations in harmony with nature. The garden, as an integral part of daily living, offers a meaningful way to reestablish, enhance, and preserve a healthful balance between humankind and the larger living community. This idea is not new, but emerged with the advent of the Arts and Crafts Movement in the mid-eighteenth century, when the negative potential of technology became apparent and the fragility of natural systems was first glimpsed.

In both England and North America, the Arts and Crafts Movement developed in reaction to the homogenizing forces of the Industrial Revolution and to Victorian society's penchant for exoticism and ostentatious display. The new machines were diminishing individual freedom in the workplace, and their potential for uniform mass production had begun to undermine the regional expression that was traditional to various arts and crafts.

Beginning in 1851 in London, international exhibitions displayed the latest products and inventions. Horticulture was prominently represented, but with little relation to locale. The great Crystal Palace, built for the London exhibition, was filled with tender tropicals imported from exotic habitats. Visitors to the 1876 Centennial Exhibition in Philadelphia could view a similar tropical palette inside Horticultural Hall or marvel at beds of brilliantly colored tropical annuals arranged in strict geometrical patterns outside the building. Chicago's 1893 Columbian Exposition included vast halls dedicated to Machinery and Electricity, in which everything from steam generators to phonographs, telephones, and incandescent light bulbs were demonstrated. These machines could, as promised, turn night into day for all practical purposes. They could also, unfortunately, turn day into night. The discharge from coal-fired factory smokestacks literally blackened the noon skies of many industrial cities, provoking the original flight to the suburbs.

Though modern machines seem more subtle in their influence, they present new potential to displace nature from our everyday existence: fabulous as it is, the internet-connected computer is a much more pervasive force than the mechanical typewriter or the fountain pen before it. The modern dilemma was neatly summarized by David Abram in the Winter 1996 issue of *Orion* magazine, which focuses on the relationship of people and nature. In his essay "Turning Inside Out: Remembering the Sensuous Earth," he suggests that "the ability to interact with our own signs in utter abstraction from our earthly surroundings has today blossomed into a vast, cognitive realm, a horizonless expanse of virtual interactions and encounters. In contrast to the...global character of the technologically mediated world, the sensuous world...is always local." A respect for local character and a joy in the sensual delights of our earthly surroundings was central to Arts and Crafts ideals, and many period notions for conserving these things are as worthy today as they were a century ago.

THE IDEA OF NATURE

Debate concerning our ideal relationship to nature certainly preceded the Arts and Crafts Movement. Some philosophers naively considered nature to be all-powerful, all-knowing, all-good. Others understood nature as a complex system subject to human influence and interpretation. Ralph Waldo Emerson, whose writings influenced many Arts and Crafts personalities, including Charles Greene and Frank Lloyd Wright, wrote in his book *Nature* (1836): "Not the sun or the summer alone but every hour and season yields its tribute of delight; for every hour and change corresponds to and authorizes a different state of mind from breathless moon to grimmest midnight."

The majority of Arts and Crafts period garden-makers were trained primarily in related arts, such as architecture or painting, and their sensibilities generally reflected this background. They looked to nature for inspiration, but had confidence that the garden was not merely a replication of nature but a work of art clearly reflecting human influence. In *Wood and Garden* (1899), renowned British gardener and garden writer Gertrude Jekyll (1843–1932), whose earliest ambition was to be a painter, stated "though no artificial planting can ever equal that of nature," gardeners could learn from observing nature "the importance of moderation and reserve, of simplicity of intention, and directness of purpose, and the inestimable value of the quality called 'breadth' in painting. For planting ground is painting a landscape with living things; and as I hold that good gardening takes rank within the bounds of the fine arts, so I hold that to plant well needs an artist of no mean capacity." Numerous other Arts and Crafts period writings underscored the importance of careful observation. *The Studio*, a widely read and internationally influential magazine, published a 1912 article titled "On the Value of Observation," which stated that "Nature is infinite in her variety," and suggested that the only way to maintain a vitality in creative work was to observe nature "continuously and conscientiously."

Arts and Crafts details on the buildings
and grounds of the Carson Valley School in
Flourtown, Pennsylvania, reflect the belief in
the good influence of the beautiful.

LEFT: A Gothic arch fashioned from local
stone leads to a student residence.

ABOVE: Tile from the nearby Enfield Pottery
and Tile Works was specially crafted for
various uses throughout the campus. Still in
superb condition today, a beautifully detailed
tile depicting a thistle greets students entering
Thistle Cottage.

Coupled with the reverence for nature was the belief in the positive influence of the beautiful. Arts and Crafts thinkers from William Morris to Gustav Stickley to Frank Lloyd Wright believed that natural beauty incorporated into daily surroundings promoted healthy, moral living and provided an antidote to the societal ills associated with the industrial age. This notion sometimes transcended the individual's garden, and Arts and Crafts decorative themes and motifs were often adopted by public institutions such as parks, schools, and libraries.

DEFINING THE ARTS AND CRAFTS GARDEN

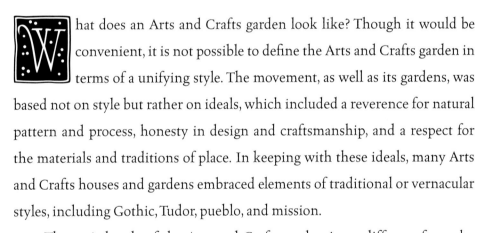hat does an Arts and Crafts garden look like? Though it would be convenient, it is not possible to define the Arts and Crafts garden in terms of a unifying style. The movement, as well as its gardens, was based not on style but rather on ideals, which included a reverence for natural pattern and process, honesty in design and craftsmanship, and a respect for the materials and traditions of place. In keeping with these ideals, many Arts and Crafts houses and gardens embraced elements of traditional or vernacular styles, including Gothic, Tudor, pueblo, and mission.

The varied style of the Arts and Crafts garden is no different from the movement's varied style in architecture and decorative objects. Though Gustav Stickley's plain oak furniture is sometimes said to typify Arts and Crafts style, it is no more faithful to the ideals of the movement than the beautifully detailed furniture of William Morris or the carved pieces of Ernest Gimson or Charles and Henry Greene. The bungalow often expressed Arts and Crafts ideals in architecture, but so did the visually distinct building styles of Edwin Lutyens and Charles Lummis. French statesman Chateaubriand, who traveled to North America in the late eighteenth century, observed:

Simple and honestly wrought, the hand-carved side panels of an L. & J.G. Stickley library table depict overlapping leaves. More than a matter of style, Arts and Crafts ideals placed the highest value on integrity of craftsmanship and design.

"Ideas can be, and are, cosmopolitan, but not style, which has a soil, a sky, and a sun all its own." Of all artistic works, it seems most obvious that the style of a garden should reflect the nature of place.

Though the style of Arts and Crafts gardens varies, there are a number of characteristics that can be identified:

❧ A UNITY OF HOUSE AND GARDEN. The holistic approach of the Arts and Crafts Movement called for a graceful, gradual transition from house to garden, often extending to the wild landscape beyond. This was achieved in many different ways. Most often, the interior spaces of the dwelling opened onto garden "rooms" defined by stone or masonry walls, trellis screens, hedges, or alleys of trees. The formality of these garden spaces was usually greatest near the house, graduating to more informal enclosure at the periphery.

Architectural elements also served to connect house and garden. Pergolas, either freestanding or attached to the house, were frequently employed as a means of providing a structured journey from the house to the outer areas of the garden. Sometimes a central courtyard, planted and open to the sky, was designed into the core of the house. Windows, often many and large, offered carefully choreographed views of the garden or the adjacent landscape. Planter boxes or troughs were frequently integrated into the dwelling, built directly into walls or porch overhangs.

Decorative items and materials were typically used to link interior and exterior spaces. Interior furnishings from furniture to tiles, metalwork, wallpaper, or paintings evoked themes from nature or sometimes borrowed motifs directly from the house's garden. In the garden, crafted elements including tiles and planter pots continued the link.

Planter boxes designed by architects Charles and Henry Greene are integral parts of the great sleeping porches of the Gamble House in Pasadena, California. The Greenes routinely sought such simple but ingenious ways to link house and garden.

NATURE AS PRIMARY SOURCE.

Nature was considered a powerful force for goodness and beauty, and observations of natural materials, patterns, and processes provided the main source of artistic and practical inspiration. Influential Arts and Crafts architect C.F.A. Voysey summarized the reverence for nature in a 1909 lecture, suggesting "Everywhere we find her making the best possible use of immediate conditions, evolving beauty out of fitness, and wisdom out of regard for requirements, materials, and conditions, all in exquisite harmony." This ideal shares much with modern notions of conservation of natural resources.

USE OF LOCAL MATERIALS, OFTEN EXTENDING TO THE PLANTS THEMSELVES.

Whenever practical, materials native or traditional to the region were used in the construction of houses and gardens to preserve the inherent sense of place. Gertrude Jekyll and Lawrence Weaver's 1912 book, *Gardens for Small Country Houses*, clearly expressed these ideals. The authors recommended studying the natural conditions of the site before beginning design of house or garden. They recognized that not every site has distinct natural character, but when such character does exist, it is the site's most

ABOVE LEFT: *The yellow lotus (Nelumbo lutea) is a Florida native long revered by local Indians for its majestic beauty and edible tubers.*

ABOVE RIGHT: *The native lotus directly inspired the central motif in the tower floor tile mural at Bok Tower Gardens in Lake Wales, Florida. Nature, especially local nature, often served as design inspiration for Arts and Crafts architecture, decorative objects, and landscapes.*

OPPOSITE: *Common, simple plants were frequently celebrated in Arts and Crafts decorative objects and gardens. The overlay on this Silver Crest vase is remarkably true to the form and graceful beauty of these native cattails (Typha latifolia).*

A HARMONY OF HOUSE AND GARDEN

Choose interior furnishings that reflect the colors and patterns that naturally occur in the regional landscape and in your own garden. The warm beauty of quarter-sawn oak furniture, for instance, enhances the house's connection with local trees and natural earth tones. The soft blues and greens of matte-finished vases and bowls and in hand-woven vegetable-dyed rugs direct the eye to similar colors in nature such as the tints and tones of the sky, of local waterways, of lichen-encrusted rocks, or of natural carpets of moss. Decorative motifs on ceramics and linens were often directly inspired by local plants. Seek out artworks that reveal and celebrate the beauty of plants or other natural features in your region.

precious quality and one that should be carefully maintained and fostered. When considering the choice of architectural materials, they believed that if a suitable local stone existed, it was the best thing that could be used. Plants that were locally native or representative of local tradition were seen as key to keeping the regional character. Jekyll and Weaver described beautiful wild places in England, including moorlands with their heaths and heathers, and called them "natural gardens" that could be conserved within the designed landscape. They deplored the destruction of regional

Charles Fletcher Lummis built his home of local boulders carried from the nearby arroyo, and nestled it among the native sycamores that provide the essential character of the place.

beauty through "commonplace treatment," going so far as to suggest that the "consistent and harmonious planting" in such wild places could not be improved by "any choice from a nursery catalog." A reverence for big trees, singly or in characteristic groves, was also commonly displayed in period Arts and Crafts gardens.

Although the science of ecology was virtually unknown in their day, Jekyll and Weaver approximated some of its basic tenets by recognizing that natural conditions such as soil type and underlying rock influenced which plants would perform best in a particular area. Gardeners who were careful observers would see that each region has its own "classes of trees and plants that will best flourish and best adorn." By working with the natural restrictions on plant choices dictated by natural conditions, gardeners would find their work easier and would realize "possibilities that are delightful." They did not suggest that gardens must be restricted only to regional native plants, but rather that these "should be well represented, and give the note to the whole arrangement."

An enthusiasm for old-fashioned plants such as hollyhocks, shrub roses, and narcissus was evident in a majority of Arts and Crafts gardens. Their use was motivated by a nostalgia for the perceived purity and simplicity of earlier times and by a desire to hold on to rural garden traditions, as well as a practical realization that old-fashioned plants were often simply stronger and easier to grow. Highly bred florist varieties and double-flowered types, associated with Victorian excess, were generally frowned upon.

Also in keeping with the preservation of tradition, many Arts and Crafts gardens included an orchard or

Hollyhocks grace a stone wall in Chipping Campden, not far from C.R. Ashbee's original Guild of Handicraft. The simple, architectural beauty and easy culture of hollyhocks has endeared them to countless Arts and Crafts gardeners from William Morris to Frank Lloyd Wright.

LEFT: *William Morris' Red House was originally set in an established orchard, as shown in this image from* The Studio *magazine of October 15, 1900.*

BELOW AND OPPOSITE: *A hedge of clipped yews and a straight stone walk provide formal frameworks for the naturalistic, flowing herbaceous borders at Great Dixter.*

at least some planting of fruit-bearing trees. The orchard was valued for the basic sustenance it provided, for its beauty, and, particularly in England, for its link to medieval gardens.

◑ FREEDOM OF GROWTH IN THE PLANTINGS. Although the basic architecture and design of Arts and Crafts gardens frequently included formal elements such as axes and symmetry, the plants themselves were typically loose and naturally flowing. In this regard, Arts and Crafts gardens represented a harmonization of two different schools of thought, the "formal" versus the "natural." Gertrude Jekyll was influential in promoting this marriage between formal layout and naturalistic plantings, believing these designs to be less costly than the rigid bedding schemes popular in Victorian gardens.

Many Arts and Crafts gardeners, most notably William Robinson, author of *The Wild Garden* (1870), embraced the notion of allowing plants to self-sow and naturalize, especially in garden areas slightly removed from the house. In apparent contradiction to all this were the finely clipped yew hedges and plants trained on trellis screens that were especially popular in British Arts and Crafts gardens. These formal practices dated to the medieval period in England, which was held as an example of a purer, simpler time by Arts and Crafts philosophers from A.W.N. Pugin to John Ruskin to William Morris.

𝒸 **NATURALISTIC COLOR SCHEMES.** Although they could be quite colorful at times, Arts and Crafts gardens generally embraced the more subtle hues and color cycles found in nature, and disdained the static, exaggerated palette of the Victorian garden. As William Robinson put it in his book *The English Flower Garden:* "Nature is a

BIRTH OF A MOVEMENT

Nature's color sequences are among the unique signatures of place.

OPPOSITE: *In regions characterized by deciduous woodlands, the season begins with a myriad of greens.*

BELOW LEFT: *Soft pastels such as blue phlox* (Phlox divaricata) *harmonize with this verdant background.*

BELOW RIGHT: *Later, the summer sun is met by warm vibrant colors such as the golden yellow of cup-plant* (Silphium perfoliatum).

good colorist, and if we trust to her guidance we never find wrong colour in wood, meadow or on mountain."

Green, the primary color of natural landscapes, was seen not merely as background, but as one of the most important colors in the garden. British architect C.F.A. Voysey advocated taking cues directly from nature's colors and sequence, observing: "She furnishes with an abundance of the most soothing color—green. She uses her red most sparingly. In the spring she feasts us with delicate greens, greys, purples, and later on, yellow, gradually warming and strengthening her color as the summer sun increases its power over the eye…nature never allows her colors to quarrel…. Harmony is everywhere."

CELEBRATING REGIONAL RHYTHMS AND MATERIALS

Take time to observe and appreciate the natural colors and sequences unique to your region, then use these observations as a basis for your garden designs and plantings. Celebrate both the vibrant moments and the quiet periods. For example, areas within deciduous woodlands are naturally the most colorful in spring when wildflowers bloom and in autumn when asters and goldenrods join a kaleidoscope of brilliant foliage. Summers are typically green and shady, and winter's tones are subtle and soft. Design your garden to embrace and emulate these cycles. The resulting landscape will reflect a genuine harmony with nature.

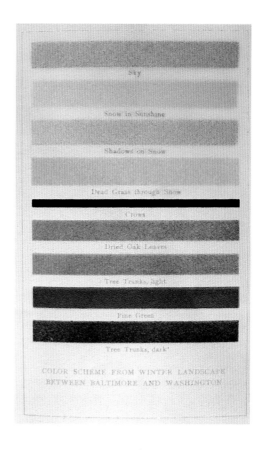

COLOR SCHEME FROM WINTER LANDSCAPE
BETWEEN BALTIMORE AND WASHINGTON

LEFT AND ABOVE: *All native landscapes have a season where color is at its lowest ebb but there is still considerable beauty apparent to the trained eye. A chart from Emily Noyes Vanderpoel's book* Color Problems *displays typical colors of an eastern North American winter landscape. This simple device helps to reveal the subtle hues in a Delaware beech forest in February.*

The drama of this planting at Hestercombe derives primarily from the contrast between the bold rounded leaves of Bergenia *and the narrow linear foliage of* Miscanthus sinensis *'Gracillimus'.*

In keeping with the artistic sensibilities of the movement, Arts and Crafts gardeners and painters alike sought to observe and emulate the variation in seasonal color and mood evidenced in nature. In *Color Problems: A Practical Manual for the Lay Student of Color* (1903), Emily Noyes Vanderpoel demonstrated how artists could celebrate nature's colors, including the subtle hues of winter. Also in keeping with the holistic spirit of the Arts and Crafts Movement, the study of natural color was not restricted to plants, but also looked to the native fauna for inspiration.

❧ PLANTS VALUED FOR FOLIAGE CHARACTER AS WELL AS FLOWERS.

In contrast to the Victorian view of plants solely as "flowers on stems," the broader emphasis of the Arts and Crafts garden placed a high value on other aspects, including form and foliage texture. Again, this emphasis developed from a respect for natural patterns, as expressed by British Arts and Crafts architect Edward S. Prior (1852–1932) in 1889: "There are Nature's own Textures for us to use…we may borrow from her and show the natural grain and figure of her work."

Though plants were extremely important to the Arts and Crafts concept of the garden, the mere acquisition and collecting of plants was not allowed to drive the design. The focus on novelty and the constant quest for exotic introductions typical of Victorian gardens was seen as superficial and contrary to the making of a harmonious landscape.

Period Arts and Crafts gardens also sought to recognize and capture many of nature's incidental delights, such as shadows, reflections, fragrances, and the sounds of wind and water. Jekyll and Weaver pointed out the simple satisfactions of tall trees flecking a path "with sunlit tracery."

THE TRANSITION FROM ENGLAND TO NORTH AMERICA

Arts and Crafts gardens in the British Isles and in North America were born of the same basic philosophy; they varied, however, in response to the unique histories, opportunities, and challenges of the different locales. The English wilderness had vanished long before the coming of the Industrial Revolution. There, the movement was more a

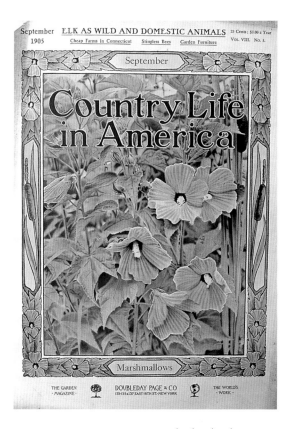

ABOVE AND RIGHT: *Closely related to hollyhocks, North American marsh mallows* (Hibiscus moscheutos) *were featured on the September 1905 cover of* Country Life in America.

response to a loss of crafts traditions and a desire to return to the simpler existence and intimacy with nature symbolized by rural cottage life. In America, industrialization coincided with the closing of the last frontiers and a sense of lost wilderness, and the garden was more often seen as a way to hold on to a bit of wild nature. As might be expected from a movement that revered regional character, the vast difference in native conditions between the two countries also resulted in different expressions of the Arts and Crafts garden.

Despite the fact that transportation and communications technologies were relatively primitive compared to today, there was a great deal of discussion between Arts and Crafts proponents in different countries. British magazines such as *The Studio, Country Life,* and William Robinson's *The Garden*

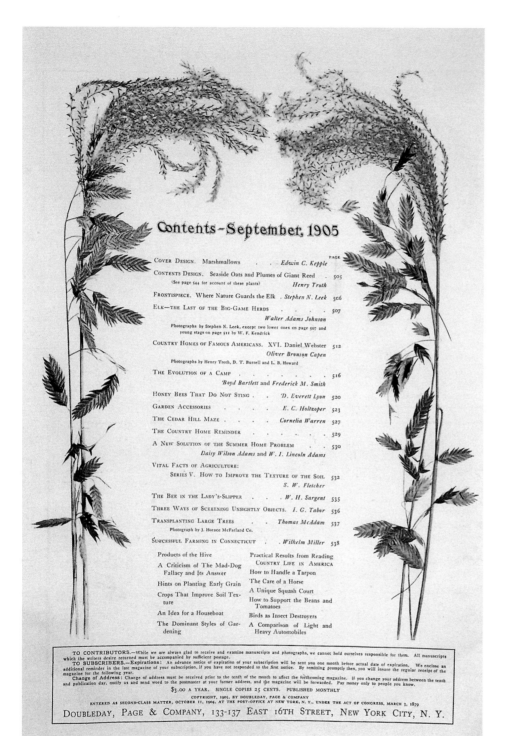

The graceful beauty of ornamental grasses was appreciated by Arts and Crafts period gardeners and promoted by magazines such as Country Life in America, *which featured* Miscanthus *and sea-oats (*Uniola paniculata*) on its contents page for September 1905.*

routinely included articles on Arts and Crafts philosophy and landscapes, and were known to Arts and Crafts leaders in North America. Arts and Crafts gardens were featured in America's own publications, including *Country Life in America, House and Garden, The Ladies Home Journal, House Beautiful,* and Gustav Stickley's *The Craftsman,* and many of these influenced British thought. Wilhelm Miller served both as editor of *Country Life in America* and as associate editor of Liberty Hyde Bailey's monumental *Cyclopedia of Horticulture,* the standard reference for turn-of-the-century American gardeners. Miller's interest in landscape theory related to the Arts and Crafts Movement was reflected in both publications.

Even at the end of the nineteenth century, ocean liners permitted a fair amount of visitation among the international Arts and Crafts community. Gustav Stickley and Charles Greene both made trips to England to learn about the Arts and Crafts Movement. C.R. Ashbee of Chipping Camden in the British Cotswolds visited Charles Greene in California and Frank Lloyd Wright in Wisconsin. Wright returned the visit, and he and Ashbee continued a friendly exchange for decades.

Despite the fact that they sprang from similar motivations and shared philosophies, Arts and Crafts gardens in England and North America are often quite distinct in style and detail. Each country offered unique opportunities and challenges that had a profound impact on the gardens. A number of the best survive, and they are rich with insights for modern gardeners.

Part Two

THE ARTS AND CRAFTS GARDEN IN ENGLAND

Edwin Lutyens incorporated an old millstone into the south landing at Little Thakeham and filled its center with bits of roof tile.

LEFT: *The pergola at Little Thakeham creates a seamless transition from house to garden. The far end offers a view over orchards to the woodlands beyond.*

OPPOSITE: A carefully crafted vista stretches between garden rooms at Little Thakeham, designed by Edwin Lutyens. Dramatically positioned on axis with the walk, a pedestalled planter serves as a focal point and invites strollers to experience another room in the garden.

A love of nature had long been a British national characteristic, and the mechanization of life that resulted from the Industrial Revolution was seen as threatening the presence of nature in everyday life, particularly in the city. The crafts tradition, also seen as basic to British character, was quickly eroding in the face of industrial competition. By the mid-nineteenth century, many urban dwellers were longing for a healthier, more natural existence. This was idealized as a rural life devoted to traditional crafts, where the free-flowing nature of the traditional cottage garden was encompassing and comforting.

A number of social critics took up the cause, with art critic and philosopher John Ruskin (1812–1900) prominent among them. Ruskin held that "dreaming," "earthiness," and "sensuality" were the "glowing moments" of human existence, and that it was critical not to lose these qualities of life to mechanization. He believed that machines robbed labor of its nobility, its freedom, and its individuality, and he preached widely against the machine and in favor of a social system modeled on medieval guilds, in which he imagined workers living a more noble life, free to express themselves in their work. Following the earlier writings of architect and theorist A.W.N. Pugin (1812–1852), Ruskin also promoted Gothic style as most appropriate for English architecture. Like Pugin, he argued that medieval Gothic was honest and straightforward in its design, unlike the Neoclassical style that was in vogue in Victorian society. Though Ruskin inspired a number of followers, most

NATURAL FREEDOM IN PLANTINGS

Whether your garden is formal or informal in its layout, take advantage of plants' natural tendency to fill and flow. Plan your garden so that plants may lean gently against one another and drift over walkways and other architectural elements. Many perennial sages, including Artemisia spp. and Salvia spp., naturally form low, spilling mounds and are ideal for such purposes. The flowing forms of ornamental grasses such as fountain grass (Pennisetum spp.) and blue lyme grass (Leymus arenarius) were similarly appreciated by period Arts and Crafts gardeners for their casual sensuality.

Design paths of sufficient width to allow for both plants and people. Four-to six-foot (1.2–1.8m) path widths are ideal.

Celebrate serendipity: welcome plants that will self-sow modestly into available niches. They will naturally choose spots that afford ideal cultural conditions, and will be better adapted and more enduring. Old-fashioned single-flowered hollyhocks (Alcea rosea) grow readily from seed and naturalize easily in the garden. Many North American native wildflowers naturalize readily. Eastern gardeners might try various asters (Aster spp.), while gardeners in arid regions might choose California poppies (Eschscholzia californica) or desert globe mallows (Sphaeralcea spp.).

*An artful ensemble of hardy perennials
tumbles gently onto a native stone walk in a
contemporary cottage garden in the rural
English village of Sapperton.*

notably William Morris, his naïve and absolute resistance to the machine was clearly unsuccessful. Ruskin's influence in the garden was much more profound, since his vision of nature as the primary source of artistic inspiration was taken up directly by William Morris, Gertrude Jekyll, William Robinson, and eventually by countless others. Even in the modern technological world, the garden has ultimately proved one of the most widely accessible mediums for individual expression.

The Arts and Crafts garden in England predates its North American counterparts, with William Morris' Red House (1859) widely acknowledged as the first. Red House and many other early British Arts and Crafts gardens were highly architectural, which is not surprising since many of the people influential in its conception (including Morris) were trained as architects. Urbanization, more advanced in England than in America, created a greater desire for the garden as a refuge from modern life, often achieved through the formal enclosure of masonry walls. Gertrude Jekyll maintained that walled forecourts provided the experience of "stepping into another world—a comforting world of sympathetic restfulness that shuts out all bustle and hurry, and induces a sense of repose and invigorating refreshment."

The concept of "wild gardening," based on the use of hardy perennials often naturalized under native trees, originated in England and was articulated and promoted by William Robinson in *The Wild Garden*. Arts and Crafts gardeners who embraced this idea were likely to let plantings, rather than walls, define garden spaces, especially at the periphery. Though Robinson and others championed the use of England's indigenous plants in the garden, they were rarely exclusive in this regard, and were equally welcoming of species from other lands if the plants were readily adapted to the English climate and natural conditions.

ABOVE: *The flying buttresses and Gothic arches of Malmesbury Cathedral typify the medieval style that Pugin and Ruskin promoted as most appropriate for England.*

OPPOSITE: *Free-flowing plantings clothe garden walls at Little Thakeham, making generous use of bold, architectural plants such as bear's-breech (Acanthus mollis). Plantings also soften the hard edges of masonry, and ease the transition from garden room to room.*

RED HOUSE

Though William Morris (1834–1896) is best remembered today for his extraordinary contributions to decorative design, encompassing everything from wallpaper to printing to furniture, his true lifelong passion was social change. He believed implicitly in a unity of the arts, and saw the garden as basic and essential to balanced good living. In his utopian novel *News from Nowhere* (1890), Morris pictured an England in which factories and cities had disappeared and the country had become one continuous garden. This enticing vision was never realized, but Morris' own first garden at Red House (1859) in Bexleyheath provided him opportunity to test many of his ideas in a personal way. The house and its gardens have survived to inspire generations seeking an understanding of Morris' vision.

William Morris' profound appreciation of nature may be traced to his boyhood, during which he spent countless days exploring Epping Forest, which was adjacent to the family estate in Essex. Though exceptionally gregarious as an adult, Morris as a youth enjoyed many solitary hours in first-hand observation of nature. His exceptional visual memory captured myriad details that were later to serve as source material for his design work. His vivid imagination was also fueled by visits to old buildings and churches, and by books such as Sir Walter Scott's novels, which depicted an earlier, simpler time in English history. Together, these things generated in Morris a deep empathy for the traditional English landscape.

Red House, conceived in 1858 and built the following year, was more than just Morris' home. It was an attempt to forge a new model of living in which house and garden were one, unified by a love of nature, a respect for

A majestic English oak (Quercus robur) grows wild in England's Lake District. A desire to conserve and celebrate England's native forests and natural landscapes was shared by William Morris and many other founders of the Arts and Crafts Movement.

NATURAL FREEDOM IN PLANTINGS

Climbing vines can play a major role in the free-flowing naturalism of the garden. High-climbing roses or sweet autumn clematis bring delightful fragrances to upper-floor windows, porches, and balconies. Trumpet honeysuckles such as North American native *Lonicera sempervirens* are certain to draw hummingbirds into close view. Forms are available with flower colors from deep scarlet to sulphur yellow, and none have the invasiveness of Japanese honeysuckle (*Lonicera japonica*). North American native wisterias (*Wisteria frutescens* and *Wisteria macrobotrys*) are delightful, diminutive alternatives to Asian wisterias.

tradition, and the artistic contributions of a community of friends. Morris invited his friend Philip Webb (1831–1915), who was to become one of England's most influential Arts and Crafts architects, to design the house. The two worked together intimately to marry the design of house and garden, and were joined by Morris' other artist friends, including painters Dante Gabriel Rosetti and Edward Burne-Jones, in decorating the interiors of Red House.

Both Morris and Webb subscribed to the moral and philosophical influence of Pugin and Ruskin. Built of red brick (hence the name) with a tile roof, Red House included in its design elements of English vernacular style mixed with Gothic. Although no pergolas or porches extended from the house, the basic L-shaped plan of the building formed a partly sheltered courtyard that included a picturesque well.

In a number of ways, the gardens at Red House represented Morris' idealized medieval garden, which was characterized by orchards, trellises, and walls. Red House was built on the site of an existing orchard, carefully conserved during construction so that it became a major element of the finished garden. Fruiting species in the orchard included apple, pear, plum, damson, and quince. A high red brick wall separated the garden from the adjacent country lane, and many of the interior garden spaces were defined by trellises or by clipped hedges. Though much of the basic layout was formal, Morris softened all the edges with plantings of old-fashioned flowers, including his favorite hollyhocks and climbing roses, as well as delicate native species, such as common primrose (*Primula vulgaris*), honeysuckle (*Lonicera periclymenum*), wood anemone (*Anemone nemorosa*), and wild strawberry (*Fragaria vesca*). Many elements and patterns from the plantings at Red House were captured in Morris' and his friends' decorative artwork, which helped to bring the garden into the interior of the house.

OPPOSITE, TOP AND BOTTOM: *In the Well Court of William Morris' Red House, mixed vines grow freely up the red brick walls toward the distinctive circular windows. The windows' interiors were decorated in floral motifs by Morris and his friends.*

BELOW: *The sturdy spires of hollyhocks grace a Gothic arch at Red House.*

Red House included a great number of windows, some decorated with nature motifs, others offering unobstructed views of the garden. The basic Gothic style of the house was not, however, compatible with glassed sun-rooms or arbors connecting directly to outdoor garden spaces. These devices came later in the development of the Arts and Crafts garden.

Morris in many ways became the voice and conscience of the Arts and Crafts Movement in England. His explorations with Red House and its gardens firmly established that landscape art and stewardship were essential to the ideal.

RODMARTON MANOR

Of all the great Arts and Crafts period gardens, Rodmarton Manor, near Cirencester in the Cotswolds, represents the purest commitment to the use of local materials and belief in the nature-affirming simplicity of traditional ways. Built over a period of twenty years beginning in 1909, Rodmarton is a defiant statement against industrialization, built only of local materials without any assistance from power machinery. Every stone and piece of slate was quarried nearby, transported in farm carts, and then cut, shaped, and put in place by local masons. All the carpentry and joinery was done by local craftsmen using wood that had been felled and seasoned on the estate. The furniture, much of it designed by Ernest Gimson, was also made on site.

Rodmarton was built for Claud Biddulph and his wife, Margaret, who was a knowledgeable horticulturist. Ernest Barnsley (1863–1926) served as primary architect for the house and worked together with Rodmarton's head gardener William Scrubey and with Mrs. Biddulph on the design of the garden. Barnsley, a disciple of Philip Webb, had come to the Cotswolds seeking a simpler way of life in the country. He built his own home and

OPPOSITE: *Rodmarton Manor represents a thorough commitment to local materials and traditions. The house and garden elements were built of stone and slate from local quarries, and trees from the estate were felled to provide wood for the structural beams of the house and for interior millwork and furnishings. All work was done by local craftsmen.*

OVERLEAF: *The solid mass and bold forms of farm relics play against clipped topiary in a garden room at Rodmarton Manor. Stone watering troughs have here been recycled as impressive planters.*

garden, called Upper Dorvel House, from an existing cottage in the nearby village of Sapperton.

Barnsley saw nothing unnatural in the tradition of clipped yew hedges and topiary, and both Rodmarton and his own garden reflect his belief. The gardens at Rodmarton comprise a succession of garden "rooms" to the south and west of the manor. Some are enclosed by clipped yews, others by walls of exquisitely hand-cut local stone, and still others by rows of hornbeams or pleached lime trees. Pergolas, their sturdy crossbeams resting on columns of cut stone, also create distinct spaces within the gardens. Some spaces, such as the Long Garden, are axial and quite formal. Others, though formally enclosed, are more intimate in their mood, part of which is created by the imaginative recycling of farm relics such as watering troughs or staddle stones.

ABOVE: *Distinctive topiary is original to Ernest Barnsley's own garden at Upper Dorvel House in Sapperton.*

OPPOSITE: *In a highly stylized way, an allée of hornbeam trees at Rodmarton Manor evokes the wildness and enclosure of the English forest.*

Though Margaret Biddulph's interest in flowers was reflected in the gardens at Rodmarton, a substantial kitchen garden has always been integral to the whole. At the southwest end of the gardens, a double row of hornbeams serves as the boundary between the last formal garden room and the loosely arranged Wild Garden, a transitional space with vistas to the open country beyond.

Rodmarton stands as perhaps the purest example of a house and garden designed with regional materials and within local traditions. It also serves as a reminder that highly controlled topiary forms were once seen as part of working with nature in the garden.

GRAVETYE MANOR

The naturalistic approach to planting that is characteristic of Arts and Crafts gardens is most directly associated with William Robinson (1838–1935). Originally trained as a gardener in Ireland, Robinson adopted England as his home and enjoyed an extraordinarily successful career writing about gardens. His profoundly influential book *The Wild Garden* (1870) is still in print today, and his later work *The English Flower Garden* (1883) went through fifteen editions in Robinson's lifetime.

Like Morris, Robinson disdained the Victorian passion for carpet bedding, the practice of planting colorful tropical annuals in rigid geometric designs. Also like Morris, Robinson saw the English cottage garden, with its focus on hardy perennials and sturdy old-fashioned flowers, as much closer to nature and in keeping with England's landscape traditions and climate. Robinson considered the hothouse production of tropical annuals to be wasteful, and believed their gaudy, static color and the rigid geometry of carpet bedding designs worked directly against an awareness and appreciation

OPPOSITE: *William Robinson's Gravetye Manor was originally the home of an Elizabethan-era ironmaster. Robinson's holdings at Gravetye eventually grew to more than 1,000 acres, which he used to develop his naturalistic approach to planting.*

of nature's often subtler diversity. In *The Wild Garden*, he complained, "The passion for the exotic is so universal that our own finest plants are never planted."

Robinson promoted the naturalistic grouping of trees and flowers of field, forest, and hedgerow. His theory of wild gardening was not restricted to English native plants, but also endorsed growing "hardy exotic plants from the northern and temperate regions under conditions where they will thrive without further care." Like many modern proponents of low-maintenance naturalistic gardening, Robinson was somewhat justly criticized for going too far in his claims, but his essential message was sound: rather than tropical annuals that required expensive yearly replacement, why not make a garden of plants that could persist under England's native conditions?

Robinson did not share William Morris' nostalgia for the medieval era, but was instead motivated to celebrate what he believed to be the sensible side of English tradition, and to incorporate it into a thoroughly modern landscape ethic. Many of Robinson's ideas were compatible with those of Gertrude Jekyll, who in fact contributed the section on color in *The English Flower Garden*. Robinson was particularly concerned that the natural contours of the land be preserved in the making of the garden, and that the gardener take time to understand varying conditions such as soil type, sunlight, and moisture. These notions are all quite compatible with our modern sense of gardening ecologically.

Robinson's writings brought the theory of wild gardening to great numbers of the public in Great Britain and North America. His success allowed him in 1884 to purchase Gravetye Manor in East Sussex, originally the late Elizabethan house of an ironmaster. Robinson spent the remainder of his life at Gravetye, putting his ideas into practice. He purchased parcels of adjacent land until he owned more than 1000 acres, nearly half of which were wooded.

Robinson is often characterized as being vehemently opposed to formal gardening, but his garden was in fact a mix of formal and naturalistic plantings.

The verdant walls of Gravetye Manor blur the distinction between house and garden.

NATURAL FREEDOM IN PLANTINGS

Opportunities for free-roaming plantings vary with different regions and with various types of architecture. If left unchecked, evergreen woody vines such as English ivy (Hedera helix) can penetrate mortar joints and openings in wood shingles or siding and expose the house to moisture damage, particularly in regions with pronounced seasonal variation and high rainfall. Hardy but less woody vines such as clematis (Clematis spp.), or honeysuckle (Lonicera spp.), are often more practical alternatives. Trellises may also be used to keep vines of all sorts separated from direct contact with house walls.

Some vines offer little flowering interest, but make superb contributions to the garden through their foliage texture or seasonal color changes. North American native Dutchman's-pipe (Aristolochia macrophylla) has bold, rounded foliage that is green in summer and gold in autumn. The summer green of Virginia-creeper (Parthenocissus quinquefolia) turns vivid scarlet in autumn.

Robinson was emphatic in his disdain for clipped yews, especially in topiary form, which he ridiculed as "vegetable sculpture," but he clearly understood the need for materials, either plants or stone, that could be used to create distinct spaces. The gardens at Gravetye included many naturalistic plantings as well as a formal garden to one side of the house in which Robinson grew hybrid tea roses. The woodland garden at Gravetye, planted with thousands of naturalized perennial flowers and hardy bulbs, was widely admired in its day and was the direct inspiration for many similar gardens in England and in North America.

The existing Elizabethan architecture of Gravetye did not include any direct links to the garden such as glass-walled rooms or pergola extensions, and Robinson chose not to make any major modifications to the manor itself. The unity between the house and its gardens was instead effected dramatically with climbers and other free-form plantings that nestled against the building and partly clothed its walls. Robinson retained the orchards that predated his ownership of the estate and carefully organized the plantings at Gravetye to provide views to distant horizons.

In *Wood and Garden* (1899) Gertrude Jekyll wrote that she was in favor of "treating garden and wooded ground in a pictorial way" in order to achieve the beauty and harmony that would allow gardens to realize their ideal purpose: to provide "delight and refreshment of mind." In many ways, Robinson's gardens at Gravetye resembled a painter's conception of the idealized English rural landscape, including both cottage-type gardens and amplified versions of nature's fields and forests.

LITTLE THAKEHAM

The Arts and Crafts Movement in England was relatively mature by the time Ernest Blackburn engaged architect Edwin Lutyens to design Little Thakeham for him, and in many respects the house and its gardens embody the very best of the English Arts and Crafts garden. Built in Sussex in 1902, of stone quarried from the immediate neighborhood, Little Thakeham is a masterpiece of unified design between house, garden, and surrounding landscape.

Edwin Landseer Lutyens (1869–1944) was already renowned as one of England's most creative and capable architects, celebrated for both his larger sense of design and his unusual capacity for intimate detail. Lutyens credited his talent for appreciating both the detail and the greater pattern of a thing to

OPPOSITE, TOP AND BOTTOM: *Edwin Lutyens judged Little Thakeham to be among his best works, and it has proved to be one of the most enduring. Lutyens' skillful design connects the house and garden today just as it did when Little Thakeham was first featured in the British magazine* Country Life.

periods of ill health beginning in childhood, which kept him from traditional childhood games and instead taught him to seek enjoyment by using "my eyes instead of my feet."

By the time he began work on Little Thakeham, Lutyens had developed a solid partnership with Gertrude Jekyll, who typically designed the plantings to go with Lutyens' house and garden architecture. Jekyll, who was Lutyens' senior, is credited with encouraging the deep sense of natural materials that helped distinguish Lutyens from many other architects of his day. Together they created many houses and gardens characterized by a sensitive use of natural materials, a reverence for vernacular forms, exquisite craftsmanship, and a nature-based style of gardening. One of their celebrated works, the Deanery Garden (1899–1901), was made for Edward Hudson, who had founded the British magazine *Country Life* in 1897. Hudson became a lifelong friend and admirer of Lutyens, whose work he frequently featured in *Country Life*. Many of the gardens Lutyens and Jekyll designed together were described in *Gardens for Small Country Houses* (1912), written by Jekyll with Lawrence Weaver.

Jekyll would likely have been included in the design of Little Thakeham, except that the owner, Ernest Blackburn, was an exceptionally skilled gardener himself. Blackburn's knowledge of horticulture was significant enough that he sometimes contributed to Hudson's *Country Life*. Blackburn wanted Lutyens to design the framework for the garden, but was confident in his own ability to clothe it with

A HARMONY OF HOUSE AND GARDEN

Consider making garden rooms to create a gentle transition from the formality of the house to the naturalism of the garden. Garden walls made of materials used in the construction of the house, whether, wood, stone, or plaster, will strengthen the connection between indoor and outdoor spaces.

Masonry walls are beautiful and long-lasting, but walls of clipped shrubbery or woven materials such as willow can also be quite effective. An orderly planting of trees or shrubs can also create the sense of an outdoor room. Use flowing plantings to bring harmony between spaces, and incorporate focal points to beckon visitors into the next garden experience. A suitable focal point might be a specimen plant or an architectural element such as a ceramic planter, a fountain, or a sundial.

OPPOSITE: *Built of local stone, Lutyens' entrance forecourt at Little Thakeham begins a series of outdoor garden rooms that surround the house in a classic example of English Arts and Crafts design.*

ABOVE RIGHT: *Decorative elements including planters draw the garden stroller into each successive room, and everywhere plants soften the hard edges of architecture. Geraniums (Pelargonium hybrids) spill from a planter as lady's-mantle (Alchemilla mollis) tumbles over stone paving.*

plants. Lutyens evidently admired Blackburn's work, saying he "is really an artist...what he does is singularly good. He has made the pergola delightful...."

Lutyens sited Little Thakeham on a high point of Blackburn's property, where the land slopes gently southward from the rear of the house till it meets a large orchard. Built in Tudor style of a light-colored local stone, the house is approached from the north through a walled forecourt. This first garden room is serene and relatively shaded, filled with ferns and other plants that offer textural interest even in the absence of flowers. Arched openings in the east and west walls lead to other distinct garden spaces, with plantings becoming fuller and more flower-laden approaching the south-facing spaces to the rear of the house. Blackburn followed Robinson's naturalistic planting style, which has been followed faithfully at Little Thakeham to the present day. The sunny gardens on the south side are defined by various stone edgings and channels, with places for roses, diverse perennial plantings including lilies and irises, and a formal pool for water plants.

The pergola, which runs directly south off the rear lawn to the edge of the adjoining orchard, is perhaps the single most compelling aspect of the gardens at Little Thakeham. Sturdy and built with rustic simplicity, Lutyens' design employs massive oak beams, squared and slightly arched, laid across large pillars of roughly hewn local stone. Leading out from the house into the sun, the journey along the pergola is always naturally lit, the plantings resplendent in their translucency. The sloping ground falls away so that the south end of the pergola is fully fourteen steps above the lawn, presenting a stunning view over the continuous tops of the orchard trees to the native

BELOW: *The rear garden at Little Thakeham is filled with free-flowing plantings. Geraniums spill from an antique urn by Celtic Arts and Crafts artist Archibald Knox. Planted in a drift nearby, white lilies are traditional symbols of purity and virginity, and were frequently included in the work of pre-Raphaelite painters.*

OPPOSITE: *Lavender* (Lavandula sp.) *in a terra-cotta jar nestles into a tumbling mass of light yellow–flowered* Helichrysum.

NATURAL FREEDOM IN PLANTINGS

Though flowers were very much a part of period Arts and Crafts gardens, the greatest emphasis was on the form, scale, and textural drama of the design. The irregular forms and naturally flowing mass of herbaceous plantings make perfect textural foils for architectural elements such as pots, planters, birdbaths, and sundials.

When considering pairings of plants with architectural accents, look first at their relative shapes, sizes, and textures. Narrow, vertical plants will be most dramatic when juxtaposed with broad walls, walks, or pools. Low, loose plantings are effective in emphasizing the prominent form and dense mass common to architectural elements, while providing a graceful visual anchor to the ground.

THE ART AND CRAFT OF DESIGN

Great attention to quality in materials, craftsmanship, and design is usually evident in period Arts and Crafts gardens, and it is important to keep this in mind when creating gardens today. Seek out simple but beautiful materials that will form the framework of the garden. Use copper for gutters and flashing on garden structures, or to cap top rails of fences or pergolas; copper weathers to blue-green tones that meld gently with plantings. Construct wooden joints in garden architecture using mortise and tenon methods, as employed in Arts and Crafts furnishings. Recycle sturdy materials such as ceramic roof tiles or cut stone paving from earlier houses or landscapes, especially those that echo the history or traditions of your region.

woods at the distant edge. This arrangement represents perfectly the English Arts and Crafts ideal of formality near the house gently dissolving and eventually meeting with nature uncontrived and uncontrolled.

Lutyens' design for the interior of the house is equally inspired. The Tudor exterior style allowed him to place generous windows in all the main rooms, offering views to the gardens outside and below. He located the dining room, drawing room, and main living hall to the rear of the house, and ornamented them with great expanses of glass looking out to the gardens. The view from the main hall was further enhanced by a two-story bay that projected south on axis with the pergola. In addition to offering a steady visual link with the garden, orchard, and woodlands, the south-facing aspect ensured that the main rooms of the house would constantly reflect the fleeting moods of the sun, the moon, and the passing seasons.

Little Thakeham was enjoyed for many years by the Blackburn family, and is fortunately in the present-day stewardship of the Ractliff family, who appreciate both the beauty and the significance of the place. Lutyens was especially fond of his work at Little Thakeham, once proclaiming it "the best of the bunch."

OPPOSITE LEFT: *A great south-facing bay window at Little Thakeham keeps the garden constantly in view, infusing interior spaces with natural daylight.*

OPPOSITE RIGHT: *An upstairs bedroom view encompasses the south garden, the pergola, the orchard, and the distant woods.*

A WINDOW ON NATURE

Views to the garden from often-used interior spaces such as bedrooms, kitchens, dining rooms, and bathrooms are a sure way to provide a daily connection with natural events and rhythms. Consider this connection when designing, siting, or modifying your house or garden.

Modern windows and window-doors offer the opportunity to enhance views without the heating and cooling losses associated with early glazing. Identify favorite interior places in the home, then enlarge or install windows or glass doors that will provide a direct view into the garden or to the surrounding natural landscape. Consider the view from indoors when laying out garden plantings, walks, or focal points.

GREAT DIXTER

Many gardens of the Arts and Crafts period were built around houses or landscapes dating to earlier times. The conservation ethic embodied in Arts and Crafts principles encouraged saving old places with distinctive character and incorporating them into sympathetic new work. Great Dixter, located in East Sussex, near Northiam, is such a place.

The core of Great Dixter is a great timber manor house that dates to the mid-fifteenth century. Nathaniel Lloyd purchased the estate in 1910 and engaged Edwin Lutyens to restore and enlarge it, and to surround it with gardens.

Lloyd was a serious student of historic architecture, and had chosen Lutyens because of his reputation for sensitive use of local materials and traditions. Together, the two made excursions around the local area studying old buildings and their landscapes. On these trips they found and purchased a long-neglected sixteenth-century manor house that retained much of its original character but was in danger of demolition. Lutyens' resulting design included the restoration of the original manor, the incorporation of the second house, and a deft linking of the two with his own architecture. Lutyens made no attempt to imitate the timber construction of the two old houses, but instead built his sections of brick and tile. He designed a series of garden spaces that literally encircled the house, erecting walls and building stairs to tie together the estate's existing farm buildings and incorporate them into a cohesive new landscape. Although he added no arbors or pergolas, his generous use of glass in the new wings offered many views of the gardens.

There were no gardens at Great Dixter at the time Nathaniel Lloyd and his wife, Daisy, acquired the property, but there were orchards and scattered trees, and these were preserved in the new design. Nathaniel Lloyd was expert in topiary, and added yews clipped in various shapes. Sometimes the yews served as great walls that acted in harmony with Lutyens' brickwork to create and organize the garden spaces. Lutyens' walls and steps display his love of fine craftsmanship, incorporating red tiling similar to that used on the roof in ways that are at once decorative and functional.

The gardens at Great Dixter represent a true mutual effort between Lutyens and the Lloyds. The Sunk Garden, enclosed both by Lutyens' walls and the sides of an old oasthouse and barn, was designed and built by Nathaniel Lloyd following the First World War. The octagonal pool at the

The entrance walk at Great Dixter leads into a half-timbered section that dates to the fifteenth century.

THE ARTS AND CRAFTS GARDEN IN ENGLAND

OPPOSITE: A *view from the roof of Great Dixter reveals the layout of various garden rooms, including the Sunk Garden.*

ABOVE: Lutyens' *design of the garden walls included his trademark attention to detail and imaginative use of simple materials such as roofing tiles.*

center has for decades been a place to appreciate the textural beauty of various water plants.

Meadow gardens, in keeping with the Robinsonian tradition, have been a significant part of Great Dixter's landscape since the Lloyds' time. Mrs. Lloyd was particularly interested in the rich tapestry of mostly native plants that will naturalize and thrive within occasionally mowed meadow grass.

Still in the care of the Lloyd family, most notably the internationally celebrated plantsman and garden writer Christopher Lloyd, the gardens at Great Dixter have evolved dramatically beyond their beginnings. The distinct char-

LEFT: *Water gardens were popular, frequent inclusions in period Arts and Crafts gardens. The Sunk Garden at Great Dixter was designed by Nathaniel Lloyd within the enclosure of Edwin Lutyens' garden walls.*

OPPOSITE LEFT: *Plantings of aquatic species such as iris, water lilies, and water-aloe* (Stratiotes aloides) *create textural drama among themselves and against the water's surface.*

OPPOSITE RIGHT: *Perimeter plantings, such as this combination of feather-reed grass* (Calamagrostis × acutiflora) *and* Eryngium × oliverianum, *are also chosen with attention to textural contrast.*

NATURAL FREEDOM IN PLANTINGS

Water gardens provide an excellent opportunity to juxtapose informal plantings with the formal edge of a pond, pool, or fountain. In addition to traditional aquatic plants such as water lilies, narrow-leaved marginal plants including cattails (Typha spp.), rushes (Juncus spp.), and sedges (Carex spp.), and numerous moisture-loving grasses such as Miscanthus, wild rice (Zizania aquatica), and giant reed (Arundo donax) will add flowing lines and graceful forms to the composition. Water gardens also add to the interest and intrigue of the landscape by reflecting the fleeting colors of the sky and the movements of clouds, sun, moon, and stars.

acter of the place continues to be celebrated and enhanced by the artistry of the gardens. A view from Lutyens' rooftop reveals that Great Dixter remains beautifully fit into the basic nature of the East Sussex surrounds.

HESTERCOMBE

Though unity of house and garden was an Arts and Crafts ideal, gardens were sometimes made distinct from the dwelling by existing circumstances. Despite this departure from the prevailing philosophy, the gardens may offer ideas and insights for today's gardener interested in the Arts and Crafts landscape legacy. At Hestercombe, in Somerset, the original Queen Anne–style house had been poorly remodeled prior to the time Edwin Lutyens and Gertrude Jekyll were brought in to create new gardens. In their design, completed in 1904, the two chose to turn their backs to the house and to make gardens compelling enough to stand alone.

Lutyens' work at Hestercombe again brings up the issue of style. Though unquestionably belonging to the Arts and Crafts period, and in many ways representative of its ideals, Hestercombe includes a great many classical details and motifs. Lutyens' career lasted well beyond the initial Arts and Crafts era, and he eventually turned away from Tudor style and vernacular tradition to embrace classical style, which became the predominant style following the First World War. Hestercombe shows early signs of this stylistic shift.

In terms of materials and plantings, the gardens of Hestercombe are fine examples of Arts and Crafts principles. Though the basic design is quite formal, the naturalism at Hestercombe was achieved by using native materials and leaving them in the natural state as much as possible. Two types of local Somerset stone made up all the garden masonry. A rough, self-splitting

OPPOSITE: *The gardens at Great Dixter meld gracefully into the surrounding countryside.*

stone was used for most of the walling, contributing a rugged beauty. For finer finished details, a strikingly different stone from the nearby Ham Hill district was used. Together the two stones create visual drama while telling something of the region's native geology.

The mortar joins of the walls were deeply raked, providing recesses in which plants could take root. Despite the considerable formality of Lutyens' garden architecture, Jekyll's naturalistic plantings brought a unifying softness

A collaboration between Edwin Lutyens and Gertrude Jekyll, Hestercombe is exquisite in its architectural and planting detail.

THE ARTS AND CRAFTS GARDEN IN ENGLAND

ABOVE: Though Lutyens incorporated a few classical styling elements in his design, he remained true to Arts and Crafts beliefs in his use of local stone.

RIGHT: Jekyll's plantings, such as this blue-flowered Ceanothus hybrid, cascaded from crevices designed into the masonry walls.

to the space. Jekyll was fond of the fine texture of ornamental grasses, including *Miscanthus,* often using them in combination with broad-leaved perennial flowers or to contrast with the hard details of stonework. A freestanding pergola was used to define the southern edge of the gardens, its lines softened by a variety of climbing vines including roses, honeysuckle, and clematis.

One of Lutyens' lingering contributions to garden design is the distinctly recognizable bench he first designed for Hestercombe. Its clean lines and sensuous, organic curves have won it a place in gardens of diverse styles and periods around the world.

The elegant fit of plantings and architecture at Hestercombe endures as an example of the combined artistry of Edwin Lutyens and Gertrude Jekyll.

OPPOSITE: Shadows play against the stonework under the freestanding pergola at the perimeter of Hestercombe's gardens.

Part Three

ARTS AND CRAFTS GARDENS ACROSS AMERICA

Mercer tile depicts leaves and acorns of the eastern North American native white oak (Quercus alba).

LEFT: *Sunlight streams through grapevines clothing the arbor at Quiet Hours, Walter Price's home and garden at the edge of Rose Valley.*

The Arts and Crafts Movement in America reached the peak of its popularity after the turn of the century, slightly later than in England. It was immensely influential and inspired a great renaissance of activity in nature-inspired decorative arts and crafts. The two settings were significantly different, however. Whereas England's arts, crafts, and architectural traditions were clearly defined, America had not yet evolved its own distinct styles. The national identity was most closely aligned with the recently vanished frontier and with the ideas of wilderness, freedom, and nature. Akin to England's Ruskin and Morris, America had its Transcendental philosophers. Preeminent among them was Ralph Waldo Emerson (1803–1882), who suggested that America develop an aesthetic derived from direct observation of nature and from the truth and substance of the American landscape. The natural garden as we still know it today grew out of such ideas coupled with the artistic sensibility of the Arts and Crafts Movement.

Gustav Stickley's magazine, *The Craftsman*, enthusiastically embraced the potential of the American garden in a June 1914 article titled "Landscape Architecture in America and its Possibilities for the Future." Here the nature of the new land was elegantly characterized: "America is richly endowed. She...inspires...by the many forms of her surfaces and the diversity of her climatic conditions. From ocean to ocean she has a wonderful flora and fauna unsurpassed in richness and adaptability." Indeed, though William Robinson's ideas on wild gardening had already taken root in America, there were no

English precedents for celebrating the vast horizontality of the American prairie, the bold forms of cacti and other desert plants, or the unique floral character of the Pacific coastal region. These would evolve as Arts and Crafts ideals were applied to the variety of American conditions.

Predictably, the Arts and Crafts Movement itself displayed a great deal of variation in America. It was never a movement based upon membership, even in England, but was rather a loose community of like-minded individuals who sought a unity in nature and the arts. Some Americans who helped shape the Arts and Crafts garden clearly identified themselves with the movement: Gustav Stickley, Will Price, and Elbert Hubbard come immediately to mind. Others, like Frank Lloyd Wright, were strongly aligned with the movement for a significant part of their careers, but would not have defined them-

A majestic native white oak spreads its branches over Gustav Stickley's Craftsman Farms in northern New Jersey. The house's green-tiled roof reflects the color of the native forest.

selves by it. Still other sectors in American culture, including American Quakerism, recognized the simple, natural values inherent in Arts and Crafts ideals and often shared or adopted them in the making of homes, communities, and landscapes. Ultimately, the combined efforts of such diverse minds and talents resulted in a great and wonderful expression of the Arts and Crafts garden in North America, as vast and varied as the continent itself.

THE AESTHETIC OF GUSTAV STICKLEY: CRAFTSMAN FARMS AND INSPIRATION FROM *THE CRAFTSMAN*

The popular appeal of Gustav Stickley's furniture often obscures his many other activities and the fact that he was the most influential proponent of the Arts and Crafts Movement in America. Writing in 1913 about the meaning of his "Craftsman Movement," Stickley (1858–1942) explained that it stood "not only for simple, well-made furniture" but also for "a distinct type of American architecture," "the companionship of gardens," and "the restoration of the people to the land and the land to the people."

Stickley's magazine, The Craftsman, published for fifteen years beginning in 1901, disseminated both Arts and Crafts philosophy and practical advice. The Craftsman brought details of William Morris and the English Arts and Crafts Movement to America, but it also routinely sought out and published Americans' experiments in adapting the ideals to regional conditions. The magazine frequently included articles on designing and furnishing houses, on the design and philosophy of gardens, and on regional landscapes and plants.

The underlying message was that much of this activity was within the means and abilities of the average person.

Stickley attempted to live this ideal at Craftsman Farms, his home in northern New Jersey from 1910 to 1917. Stickley deliberately fashioned his interiors and furnishings to evoke the native forest: in November 1911 *The Craftsman* described the "gleam of copper in the hearth-hoods, the door latches and the vases and bowls..." as evoking the woods, "brown and green with the glint of sunshine through the leaves."

Stickley followed Emerson's aesthetic principles of art derived from nature and integrity in design, which respected the inherent beauty of materials. Stickley's simplest oak pieces were the ultimate expression of Emerson's belief that unnecessary and showy details were "the ruin of any work."

Stickley was especially fond of the native white oak, admiring it as a majestic symbol of the eastern deciduous forest and for the beauty of its wood in furniture making. Stickley's straightforward designs used quarter-sawn wood whenever possible, revealing the unique figure of the grain. Expanding on the notion of "the good influence of the beautiful," he believed that the clearly expressed origins of his furniture would encourage an understanding and appreciation of the forest for its regional beauty and as a renewable resource.

The Craftsman regularly published plans for houses, and these blueprints were often accompanied by enthusiastic articles promoting the garden as an integral part of living and a critical link to nature. One such article proclaimed that "Americans have found many of the home comforts pursued so widely... are really sweetly embodied in the practical scheme of living in the midst of a garden."

The consistent message to readers was that, to achieve a true harmony with nature, the garden must evolve from the garden-maker's direct observations of natural surroundings. A 1911 issue of *The Craftsman* suggested, "A garden must be spontaneous—allowed to spring from the ground in a natural way—otherwise it is devoid of that irresistible something called style, for style

Sunlight reflected from a copper hearth hood at Craftsman Farms recalls the warm glow of the native woodlands.

is born out of the shaping of use and beauty to environment." Quite specifically, *The Craftsman* also advised: "In the question of planting…the more we know of local conditions, and particularly of the flora, the better able we are to achieve satisfactory results. It is only when a detailed study of these is made and applied…that the restful feeling of absolute harmony can be gained"

A 1914 article by Alice Lounsberry, "Bringing the Woods to the Garden," repeated this theme, suggesting: "a growing comprehension of Nature has spread over the country, her intimacy has been sought, and the desire manifested to live closely to her…." The article included recommendations of well-adapted hybrid rhododendrons, but was most progressive in its special mention of North American native rhododendrons and azaleas. Their natural habitat preferences and growing conditions were discussed, and their delicate beauty recognized: "the native azaleas R. *nudiflora* and R. *viscosum* have about them all the charm of the open country, and are…greatly to be desired for naturalistic planting."

Though more frequently focused on North American native species, *The Craftsman* confirmed William Robinson's notion that the garden would be

The white oak (Quercus alba) *is among the most majestic of North American native forest trees. It is readily grown from seed and is an excellent choice for larger private gardens, public spaces, and parks. Gustav Stickley revered the white oak for its presence in the native landscape and for the unique strength and figure of the wood in furniture making.*

RIGHT: *A cross-section of white oak reveals the prominent rays that serve to transport nutrients laterally through the living tree.*

BELOW: *When white oak is sawn parallel to the rays, the face of the sawn board displays a strikingly beautiful "ray flake" pattern. Such wood is called "quarter-sawn." The slats of this L. & J. G. Stickley Onandaga-period chair are made of quarter-sawn white oak. Gustav Stickley believed that an intimacy with native woods could contribute to the wise management of forest resources.*

more beautiful and easier to manage if it was based on plants adapted to the local conditions. A March 1913 article promoting the pleasure of water gardens suggests that readers consult their immediate neighborhoods for native shrubs, trees, and herbaceous plants growing in nearby swamps and meadows, since these "will secure a maximum of effect." The article is quite specific, mentioning moisture-loving trees including sweetgum (*Liquidambar styraciflua*), black gum (*Nyssa sylvatica*), red maple (*Acer rubrum*), and sweet-bay magnolia (*Magnolia virginiana*). It celebrates the beauty of native shrubs that are naturally adapted to wet conditions, including arrowwood (*Viburnum dentatum*), sweet pepperbush (*Clethra alnifolia*), swamp azalea (*Rhododendron viscosum*), buttonbush (*Cephalanthus occidentalis*), and winterberry holly (*Ilex verticillata*), which is promoted for the stunning winter effect of its bright red berries. Common but elegantly beautiful native plants such as cattails (*Typha latifolia* and *Typha angustifolia*) are suggested for foliage effect, and the native hibiscus is touted as "perhaps the most striking of all the native swamp plants."

Quotations from American naturalists and Transcendental philosophers were frequently invoked in support of underappreciated native plants such as asters and goldenrods. Of goldenrods, John Muir is quoted as saying "the fra-

Articles in The Craftsman *celebrated the natural beauty and garden potential of countless North American native plants.*

ABOVE LEFT: *A 1913 article described the Catawba rhododendron (Rhododendron catawbiense) as blazing "a riot of bloom throughout the Alleghenies to Georgia," and said "it is well worth traveling hundreds of miles to see as it transforms the mountainsides into huge bouquets."*

ABOVE RIGHT: *In 1914* The Craftsman *described the flowers of Carolina azalea (Rhododendron vaseyi) as "an inch and a half [5.25cm] across, and of purest pink."*

OPPOSITE, CLOCKWISE FROM TOP LEFT: *Fragrant-flowered swamp magnolia (Magnolia virginiana), native white woodland aster (Aster divaricatus), winterberry holly (Ilex verticillata), and arrowwood (Viburnum dentatum) were also featured in* The Craftsman.

grance and the color and the form and the whole spiritual expression of the goldenrod are hopeful and strength-giving beyond any flower that I know." Similarly, Thoreau says goldenrods capture "all the richness of the season and shed their mellow luster over the fields as though the now declining summer's sun had bequeathed its hues to them."

The beauty and garden suitability of native asters is also celebrated in *The Craftsman's* 1915 article "Goldenrods and Asters: Nature's Royal Embroideries of Purple and Gold." The New England aster (*Aster novae-angliae*) is termed the showiest of the wild species, but the rich diversity of natives is promoted: "there is hardly a shade of blue, purple, or lavender that is not matched by the asters."

Echoing and building on William Robinson's advice on the efficiency of naturalizing plants in the garden, *The Craftsman* suggested that "the flowers native to the place are not only the most appropriate, but take care of themselves accommodatingly, seeding themselves at the proper time." The utility of aspects beyond flowers was also valued. For example, the common bloodroot (*Sanguinaria canadensis*) was suggested as "a practical wild flower to bring into the border, since after its evanescent flowers have passed its leaves make strong clumps of green, doing service as ground covers."

The Craftsman also sought to make readers aware of the richness of the native American flora by recounting tales of its early exploration. Articles by expert authors told of the travels of pioneering botanists Asa Gray, Charles Sargent, Andre Michaux, and John Bartram. The articles celebrated the plants they discovered, such as *Franklinia*, found in Georgia by John Bartram and

ABOVE LEFT: *According to an article in the March 1913 issue of* The Craftsman: *"Dogwood blossoms bedeck the May woods as if for a festival."*

ABOVE RIGHT: The Craftsman *suggested that native goldenrods were beautiful and appropriate for North American gardens.*

OPPOSITE: *Asters, including New England aster (*Aster novae-angliae*), were also lauded by* The Craftsman *as suitable for native landscapes.*

CELEBRATING REGIONAL RHYTHMS AND MATERIALS

In many regions, including most of central and eastern North America, autumn is the most colorful time in the native landscape. This is due not just to the changing foliage of trees and shrubs, but to myriad members of the aster family, including asters (Aster *spp.*), goldenrods (Solidago *spp.*), joe-pye-weeds (Eupatorium *spp.*), sunflowers (Helianthus *spp.*), and coneflowers (Echinacea *spp.*). These species and their selected varieties can contribute immensely to the late-season glory of the garden. They are often accompanied by the brightly colored berries of native shrubs, including winterberry holly (Ilex verticillata) and spicebush (Lindera benzoin). Celebrating such autumn assemblages is a sure way of bringing the garden into a true harmony with nature.

literally rescued from extinction though its introduction to American gardens. Sounding very much like modern-day philosophy of conservation, *The Craftsman* suggested that by cultivating native plants "a step is taken toward preventing the vanishing of wild flowers."

Although articles in *The Craftsman* often reflected Gustav Stickley's familiarity with the eastern region, many described the beauty and opportunity of other areas. Regional building traditions as diverse as cave, cliff, and brush dwellings were analyzed for inspiration. The natural potential of dry-region plants was celebrated in an article titled "The Beautiful Gardens of Our Great Western Deserts." The ultimate message of *The Craftsman* was this: there is "not a bit of land where a house could be put in all this glorious land of ours that has not its colony of flowers, grasses, shrubs and trees…to grace the dooryard of their human friends."

Beyond discussing garden plants, *The Craftsman* regularly included advice on garden architecture. The pergola was consistently recommended as a harmonizing feature. A typical article of 1906, "Porches, Pergolas, and Balconies," pointed out the pleasures of outdoor rooms "always open to sun and air." Stickley himself was especially fond of the outdoor dining these spaces

ABOVE: *This illustration in the April 1912 issue of* The Craftsman *suggested the pergola as a way of framing a distant view and connecting the garden visually and intellectually to the larger landscape.*

OPPOSITE: *Charles Greene did exactly that with the pergola he designed for the Robinson garden, which looks out from the high edge of the Arroyo Seco in Pasadena.*

A WINDOW ON NATURE

A good garden can offer a wonderfully contemplative experience. There is often opportunity to frame a distant view to the hills or the sky, and to encourage quiet reflection on nature's enveloping expanse. A sense of connectedness is at the heart of Arts and Crafts ideals. The garden is a unique conjunction of art, living elements, and human events that take place in its embrace, and it has a unique ability to heal, enlighten, and inspire.

permitted. Water gardens and small pools were suggested as further ways of connecting the garden with nature's dynamic beauty, commending their ability to "catch the glow of the sky."

Many of Gustav Stickley's interior furnishings and houses survive as tangible examples of his ideals, but they are only a part of his enduring legacy. His publication *The Craftsman* remains a unique and outstanding source of inspiration and practical advice for those of us who believe in "the companionship of gardens" and a natural harmony in everyday living.

ART AND THE GARDEN: THE TILES OF HENRY CHAPMAN MERCER

True to its ideals, the Arts and Crafts Movement brought the garden closer to a unity with related arts and crafts. The renaissance in American handmade tiles had a great impact not only on houses of the period, but on gardens as well. Henry Chapman Mercer (1856–1930) of Doylestown, Pennsylvania, is rightly credited with inspiring that renaissance through the work of his Moravian Pottery and Tile Works, completed in 1912. His tiles, handmade from local clay, were widely acclaimed and found their way into Arts and Crafts houses and gardens across the country. In Pasadena, Ernest Batchelder was so impressed by Mercer's tiles that he founded his own tileworks, which also eventually won national acclaim.

Mercer loved the story-telling aspects of tiles. He designed all his own tiles, frequently borrowing stories or motifs from history and from traditional tales. Many of Mercer's tiles were made in natural earth tones and depicted native plants and animals. The tiles were often used both inside the house and in garden architecture such as gateposts, walls, and walkways.

ABOVE, LEFT AND RIGHT: *Built in 1912, Henry Chapman Mercer's Moravian Pottery and Tile Works in Doylestown, Pennsylvania, operates today as a living history museum, making tiles from Mercer's original forms.*

Fine examples of Mercer's tilework have survived in the garden and inside the small glasshouse at Willowwood, in northern New Jersey. Originally the private home of Robert and Henry Tubbs, two brothers who assembled a world-renowned collection of hardy trees and shrubs, Willowwood is now open to the public as part of the Morris County parks system.

THE ART AND CRAFT OF DESIGN

Handcrafted tiles can add depth, color, and meaning to the garden. Thanks to renewed interest in the Arts and Crafts Movement, many period tilemakers are once again in production, including Pewabic Pottery, Fulper, and Mercer's Moravian Pottery and Tileworks. The revival has also seen the birth of many new potteries that are making tiles and garden pots beautifully suited to contemporary gardens following Arts and Crafts ideals. Ceramic tiles are available in a myriad of earth and sky tones, offering unlimited opportunities for harmonious compositions with plantings. Tiles make stunning backdrops for fountains or copings on pools and water gardens, and are superb accents when inset in garden walls or walks.

ABOVE: A tile depicting the eastern gray squirrel, newly handmade from Mercer's original forms, is set into a wall of native Wissahickon schist at the Morris Arboretum in Chestnut Hill, Pennsylvania.

OPPOSITE: The Tubbs brothers chose Mercer tiles for an outdoor well (top right) and for a fountain inside a glasshouse (left and bottom right) at Willowwood, their garden and arboretum in New Jersey.

ROSE VALLEY:
AN ARTS AND CRAFTS
GARDEN COMMUNITY

One of the most enduring insights to be gleaned from Arts and Crafts ideals is that the garden can be more than just the private refuge of individuals; it can be the joint expression of a like-minded community. Many leaders of the Arts and Crafts Movement in America were strongly influenced by William Morris, had read his *News from Nowhere*, and were sympathetic to its notion that the country would ideally be one continuous garden. A number of Arts and Crafts communities were formed around the turn of the twentieth century, among them Elbert Hubbard's Roycroft community in East Aurora, New York; Ralph Whitehead's Birdclyffe, near Woodstock, New York; Will Price and Frank Stephens' Arden, near Wilmington, Delaware; and Will Price's Rose Valley, near Moylan, Pennsylvania. Though many of these communities were founded on the belief that a common dedication to arts and crafts work would bind them together, nearly all found this economically impractical in the face of increasing competition from inexpensive mass-produced goods. Some, however, found the dedication to a common landscape most sustaining, and none more beautifully so than the people of Rose Valley.

Rose Valley was primarily the conception of architect William Lightfoot Price (1861–1916), a Quaker who in 1901 purchased many acres of land in a Pennsylvania mill valley with the intent of forming a permanent community of artists and craftsmen living in simple harmony with nature. Price modified existing mill houses and designed and built new ones. He greatly admired the work of fellow Pennsylvanian Henry Chapman Mercer, and regularly used his Moravian tiles on the interiors and exteriors of the houses, as well as on the distinctive stone pillars that mark the borders of Rose Valley and many of

A *chair back hand-carved in the Rose Valley shops speaks eloquently of the crafts ideals on which the community was founded.*

its picturesque drives. Though Rose Valley's furniture, ceramics, and printing activities all ceased within a decade, the community established a tradition of gardening that continues to the present day.

One of the delightful aspects of Rose Valley, which has largely survived to the present, has to do with the sense of communal landscape. In a spirit more neighborly than socialist, the Rose Valley residents generally respected each other's freedom to travel on foot, even though such activity involved crossing what other communities might rigidly consider private property. This convention seems to echo Ralph Waldo Emerson's sentiments about the value of the common landscape. Describing a walk past neighboring farms, Emerson wrote: "The charming landscape...I saw this morning is...made up of some twenty or thirty farms. Miller owns this field, Locke that, and Manning the woodland beyond. But none of them owns the landscape.... This is the best part of these men's farms, yet to this their...deeds give no title."

The tradition of gardening runs deep in Rose Valley, and a long-standing interest in a diversity of good plants has resulted in a contemporary landscape that is particularly rich. In the early days of the community, as now, gardens

LEFT AND BELOW: *Rose Valley founder and architect Will Price used Mercer tiles on many Rose Valley houses and on distinctive masonry pillars throughout the community.*

RIGHT: *This Henry Troth photograph of an early Rose Valley water garden displays a beautiful array of plants.*

BELOW, LEFT TO RIGHT: *Some of the plants in evidence are yellow lotus (*Nelumbo lutea*), white-striped* Miscanthus sinensis *'Variegatus' and zebra grass (*Miscanthus sinensis *'Zebrinus').*

seemed to meet each other without clear boundaries. Images of some of the earliest Rose Valley gardens survive in the photography of Henry Troth, who built a bungalow in Rose Valley in 1906. Troth was a widely recognized artist whose photography, typically of landscapes and gardens, was frequently featured in national magazines, including *Country Life in America.*

Troth's images of his friend and neighbor Alice Barber Stephens' house and garden reveal a design very much in keeping with English Arts and Crafts traditions. Will Price had adapted the house from an existing barn,

A HARMONY OF HOUSE AND GARDEN

*T*he British Arts and Crafts convention of a series of garden rooms works equally well in the North American landscape. Though period gardens were often enclosed by a perimeter wall, this is only one approach. The easiest way to connect an existing house to a series of outdoor rooms is to begin with existing doorways and move outward, creating enclosure with masonry walls or wooden frameworks or with hedges or rows of trees and shrubs. Designed with careful thought, the basic architecture of the garden can survive to nurture successive generations, as walls and spaces are clothed by evolving generations of plantings.

incorporating Moravian tiles and a large studio for Stephens, who was an accomplished illustrator and photographer. Generous windows and open porches provided easy views of the landscape. As in other Arts and Crafts gardens, the plantings nearest the houses were formal, consisting of many clipped trees and shrubs. A pergola with massive stone pillars similar to those Lutyens designed led past tall sycamore trees to a springhouse, then across a neighboring drive to a pond and water garden. Many individual plants are clearly recognizable in Troth's photos, including *Miscanthus* grasses, native cattails, irises, water lilies, and the native yellow lotus. The style of the plantings around the pond is loose and naturalistic, in beautiful contrast to the finely crafted detail of the arched stone bridge.

Walter Price, Will's brother and also a gifted architect and Quaker, designed and built his own home, called Quiet Hours, in 1915 at the edge of Rose Valley. Inspired by an archway he'd seen during a trip to Tuscany, Walter Price built this feature into the enclosing wall of his new garden. The blending of indoor and outdoor space was beautifully accomplished through the use of large windows, open sleeping porches, attached arbors, and a free-standing, vine-covered pergola.

Walter Price's home and garden, Quiet Hours, just completed in 1915 (in Price's own photograph, right) and as it appears more than seventy years later (opposite).

Along the banks of Ridley Creek in adjacent Media, Pennsylvania, nurseryman Fairman Furness made his home and garden, Upper Bank, beginning in 1916. An artist as well as a plantsman, Furness lived a life true to the best of Arts and Crafts ideals. The great-nephew of noted Philadelphia architect Frank Furness, Fairman adapted and enlarged an existing eighteenth-century stone house, opening up vistas from inside and creating a series of outdoor rooms by building stone terraces up from the sloping ground. Furness was extraordinarily knowledgeable about a wide range of hardy plants, introducing many native and non-native species to cultivation through his nursery. The gardens at

BELOW: *Walter Price's design for Quiet Hours is a deft blending of indoor and outdoor space. The house and garden exist in gentle harmony.*

OPPOSITE LEFT: *Fairman Furness of Upper Bank was a keen observer of natural pattern, as seen in his watercolor of the local woods in autumn.*

OPPOSITE RIGHT: *Furness put his observations to work in crafting the architecture and plantings at Upper Bank.*

Upper Bank reflected this mix, which gradually made a graceful transition to the native flora lining Ridley Creek. Furness' artistry is evident in his plantings, in the exquisite detailing of Upper Bank's stonework, and in his paintings—dedicated to the value of observation, Furness for decades made watercolors of his developing garden and of the local fields and forests.

NATURE OBSERVED AND EMBRACED: A SYMPATHY WITH QUAKER IDEALS

The moral belief in simplicity and integrity of design that was central to Arts and Crafts ideals was also shared by other groups, including Americans of Quaker belief. In addition, Quaker ideals embraced the study of nature as a certain means of attaining a greater level of spiritual enlightenment. As a result, many Quaker buildings and landscapes overlap those of the Arts and Crafts Movement in style and substance. Mohonk Mountain House and Pocono Lake Preserve are examples of American Quaker places that illustrate a superb reverence for "nature's garden."

Mohonk Mountain House is a great country inn that sits on the rim of Lake Mohonk, surrounded by literally thousands of acres of forested mountains outside of New Paltz, New York. It was opened in 1870 by Quaker brothers Alfred and Albert Smiley, and has remained in the family's care until

BELOW AND OPPOSITE: For more than a century, the Mohonk Mountain House has promoted a quiet contemplation of nature.

OVERLEAF: Broad porches at Mohonk Mountain House offer places to sit, to talk, or to read, all while keeping nature in constant view.

the present day. As Mohonk scholar Larry Burgess has stated, the brothers shared a profound appreciation of nature, a respect for the relationship between people and their environment, and a recognition of the importance of beauty in daily life. They fashioned their Mountain House to reflect these values, and through the comfort of sympathetic architecture, to offer an easy immersion in the delights of nature. In addition to the great open verandas that provide serene places for observation, there are more than one hundred rustic shelters and viewing structures positioned along myriad paths around the lake and through the forest. Though there is a formal flower garden to one side of the inn, the greatest garden experience at Mohonk is made up of the sights, sounds, scents, and seasons of the native landscape.

Pocono Lake Preserve is a private community in Pennsylvania's Pocono Mountains begun by Quakers at the beginning of the twentieth century. Though not based on the production of art or craftwork, it is similar to Arts and Crafts communities in that it was inspired by a common reverence for nature. The communal aesthetic is one that embraces the use of local materials, colors, and quiet traditions whenever possible. This is most evident in the community approach to gardening, which is essentially to keep intervention to a minimum and to celebrate the inherent beauty of the region. This is not only an ecological choice, it is a subtly artistic one, since the natural vegetation patterns frequently result in visual drama that would be difficult to

OPPOSITE: *Houses in Pocono Lake Preserve are built of natural materials in earth tones, and the rich seasonal delights of the local woodlands are welcomed as the most beautiful of gardens.*

surpass through deliberate design. That this aesthetic has survived for nearly a century is powerful testimony to the community's nature-based ideals.

The subtle, sensible aesthetic shared by many Arts and Crafts gardens and those associated with American Quakerism suggests that William Morris' belief in the beauty of necessity can truly be a guiding ideal in the garden.

Built of local materials, more than one hundred rustic structures beckon visitors into the natural gardens that surround Mohonk Mountain House. Each structure frames a special view of the lake, forest, or the distant horizon.

CALIFORNIA EXPRESSIONS

ABOVE: *Charles Fletcher Lummis gave this distinctly dimpled boulder a prominent position in his stone chimney at El Alisal. Perhaps the stone was hollowed by the waters of the arroyo, perhaps by earlier residents, who might have used it for grinding cornmeal.*

RIGHT: *A spring carpet of native California wildflowers at Descanso Gardens includes orange California poppies (Eschscholzia californica) and desert bluebells (Phacelia campanularia). This mix evokes the kaleidoscope of color that once occurred naturally at Charles Fletcher Lummis' El Alisal.*

The Arts and Crafts Movement was exceptionally popular in early-twentieth-century California, creating a great legacy of art and architecture. Icons such as the hammered copperwork of Dirk van Erp and the "ultimate" bungalows of Greene and Greene have been justly celebrated. The gardens coinciding with these works, however, remain relatively unstudied.

At the turn of the century, many proponents of the movement were transplanted Easterners who brought with them a familiarity with Arts and Crafts gardens in England and the eastern states, and who sought to develop a new regional expression for their ideals. Some were able to see the native beauty of this essentially dry region, which is naturally full of flowers only following winter rains. Others were beguiled by the state's steady sunshine into imagining California to be a lush tropical paradise.

One of those who remained true to the Arts and Crafts ideals of working in unpretentious ways with local materials and resources was Charles Fletcher Lummis. In 1898, he built his house in Highland Park of boulders carried from the nearby arroyo and called it El Alisal, a name that referred to the enveloping grove of native sycamores. The local stone of the house rooted it firmly in the local landscape. Rather than irrigating his property to effect a semblance of the East, Lummis made his garden a celebration of the California wildflowers and native shrubs that grew naturally on his land. He reveled in his harmonious relation with California's seasonal cycles, writing in a 1905 article titled "The

RIGHT: *Pasadena tile maker Ernest Batchelder sited his house and garden among the California live oaks that clothe the edge of the Arroyo Seco.*

Carpet of God's Country": "On my own little place there are, today, at least forty million wild blossoms by calculation…you cannot step anywhere without trampling flowers—maybe ten to a step, as a minimum. One bred to climes where God counts flowers as Easterners do their copper cents may not prefer to walk on them, but out here God and we can afford the carpet."

The imagery of Pasadena's arroyos inspired the design of a number of Arts and Crafts houses and gardens. Naturally paved with huge rounded stones in meandering patterns shaped by seasonal floods and rimmed with native shrubs and majestic live oaks, the arroyo was rightly adopted as the symbol of the regional landscape.

In 1909, tile maker Ernest Batchelder built his house along Pasadena's Arroyo Seco, nestled among the native live oaks. Stones from the arroyo and various tiles set into walls, walks, and fountain are defining elements of the house and garden. The chimney at the front of the house rises from a foundation of rounded stones, and is inset with Moravian tiles. Batchelder admired and was inspired by Mercer's work, and eventually became the foremost Arts and Crafts tile maker on the West Coast. Batchelder's own tiles are featured in the fountain that provides the focal point of the rear garden.

THE GARDENS OF THE GREENES

Working within the principles shared by other California designers, the brothers Charles Sumner Greene (1868–1957) and Henry Mather Greene (1870–1954) created many gardens in association with their celebrated architecture. Echoing William Morris' sentiments, the brothers believed in a holistic approach to the design of the house, its decorative objects, and its landscape. Though their gardens often make imaginative use of design elements from Japanese or even classical gardens, the Greenes' ultimate landscape legacy is a brilliant synthesis of these and the native Cali-

Built-in planting boxes designed by Charles and Henry Greene greet visitors to the Gamble House.

fornia landscape, with its arroyos, its rugged coast, and its oak, pine, and cypress trees. In the first decade of the twentieth century, Greene and Greene designed a number of homes and gardens near one another in Pasadena. The neighborhood is very much intact to this day, and walking through it is in many ways like rambling through a continuous garden.

Built looking over the Pasadena arroyo in 1908, the David B. Gamble House is one of the brothers' acknowledged masterpieces. The integration of house, garden, and decorative details evoking the essential nature of California is exquisite. The integration of house and plantings begins immediately, with planter boxes built directly onto the front wall of the house and large urns set on the front steps and porch. The main hall is characteristically

A HARMONY OF HOUSE AND GARDEN

*A*rtworks by local craftspeople are most likely to celebrate images and events that speak of your region. Such work can be an essential part of the harmony of house, garden, and surrounding landscape. Paintings by regional artists, especially landscapes painted outdoors in the plein air tradition common to Arts and Crafts artists, will usually capture and reveal something of the local essence. Other local artisans, including metalworkers, furniture makers, and ceramicists, are excellent resources for decorative and functional items that will contribute to the regional harmony of your home. Galleries and local arts and crafts shows are superb places to look for both period and contemporary pieces.

OPPOSITE: *Views from the main hall of the Gamble House envelop the visitor in images of the California landscape. The entry mural portrays a California live oak (top). The rear view frames the garden and, originally, the adjacent arroyo (bottom).*

ABOVE AND RIGHT: *A hammered copper lamp in the main hall of the Gamble House captures the windswept essence of coastal Monterey cypress* (Cupressus macrocarpa).

beautiful. From the front, sunlight floods through a stunning Tiffany-style glass mural of the California live oak. Crafted by Emil Lange from Charles Greene's design, this mural captures the profound feelings Charles held throughout his life for California's big trees. On a table in the hall, a lamp design celebrates the Monterey cypress, native further north along the California coast. At the opposite end of the hall, wood and glass doors offer a beckoning view to the rear garden.

The low wall enclosing the rear terrace garden is built of locally made "clinker" brick, which is characteristically dark and slightly warped from extensive firing. A small pool provides space for water-loving plants, including umbrella sedge (*Cyperus alternifolius*), and mirrors the clouds and sky. The base of the terrace walls gradually give way to rounded stones from the arroyo, a device that became something of a trademark in Greene and Greene designs.

Built in the days before air-conditioning, the Gamble House has generous sleeping porches that offered both a comfortable night's rest and a closeness with the nature of California's nights. As in the front of the house, planter boxes were integral to the design of the porches. The view down to the terrace below reveals the Japanese influence in the garden, immediately obvious in the design of the copper and glass lantern.

Though the Greenes never visited Japan, they were well acquainted with the Japanese garden tradition of distilling natural patterns and processes. The rear terrace garden at the Gamble House is highly refined in its use of

masonry and native stone, in a fashion similar to that of Japanese Zen meditation gardens; its inspiration, however, is clearly the local arroyo.

Many other Greene and Greene landscapes in the neighborhood include design elements worth emulating today. Unlike earlier English Arts and Crafts gardens, the Pasadena designs of Greene and Greene frequently acknowledged the growing presence of the automobile. The driveway of the F.W. Hawks House, designed by Greene and Greene in 1906, is a veritable garden in itself. A brilliant melding of brick and stone, the drive is a highly functional abstraction of a dry stone bed in the nearby arroyo.

Even in their early designs, Greene and Greene built central garden courtyards into their houses. Some of these were simple, with earthen floors, such as the one at the Arturo Bandini House of 1903. In the Duncan-Irwin House, built in 1906, a central courtyard is visible from the dining room as it rises through two stories. Surrounded by balconies on the upper level, the space is open to the sky. Outdoor living spaces defined by arbors and pergolas were also common in Greene and Greene gardens.

Charles Greene built his own house overlooking the arroyo and shaded by native oaks in 1902, christening it Oakholm. An early black-and-white photo of majestic oaks lining a dirt lane near his house reveals his early and enduring fascination with the form and silhouette of big trees and the way sunlight plays on their structure. Charles was an admirer of Emerson's nature writings, and his sensitivity to the subtle nuances of light in the landscape grew as he matured. Two of the gardens Charles designed, made later in his career, when he was working independently of his brother, are stunningly original expressions of his artistry.

OPPOSITE TOP: *The glowing greens of a Tiffany lamp at the Gamble House bring interior space into harmony with the colors of the garden.*

OPPOSITE BOTTOM: *Rather than treat the driveway of the E.W. Hawks house as mere utility space, the Greenes made it an essential part of the garden.*

ABOVE: *Stone placement and the shape of a copper lantern at the Gamble House reflect the Greenes' admiration of Japanese styling, yet the overall design is uniquely their own.*

A WINDOW ON NATURE

Great trees can serve as framing devices in the garden, directing the eye to the colors of an evening sky, to scurrying storm clouds, or to the sensual shadow patterns of an emerging day. If there are existing trees in your garden, look for ways to build them into your design. Position a bench or a path approaching a tree so that is in line with the rising or setting sun. The trunk and branches will become stunning silhouettes, casting dramatic shadows as days pass and seasons unfold. When designing new garden spaces, consider planting an allée of trees flanking a pathway into the sunrise or sunset, or focused on a distant view.

OPPOSITE TOP: *Charles Greene's early, insightful photograph of sunlight and shadows playing through native oaks hints at his lifelong respect for great trees.*

OPPOSITE BOTTOM: *Iridescent Pewabic tiles edging the pool at the Culbertson House in Pasadena reflect and emulate the fleeting colors of the sky.*

BELOW: *A majestic California oak figures prominently in Charles Greene's garden design for the Culbertson House.*

LEFT: *Charles Greene's meticulous stonework at the D.L. James House marries the foundation imperceptibly with the native rock.*

OPPOSITE, TOP AND BOTTOM: *The most compelling aspect of the garden at the D.L. James House in Carmel is the daily opportunity to contemplate the closing of the day through a framework of Charles Greene's brilliant stonework and the natural canopy of Monterey cypress and pines.*

In 1911, Charles designed a house set high in the hills of Woodside, California, for Mr. and Mrs. Mortimer Fleishhacker. In the late 1920s, Charles was invited back to design a garden continuing down the hillside, away from the house. His design resulted in perhaps the most spectacular gardens he ever made, a brilliant melding of classical elements such as Roman arches with the coarse-textured stone and rugged native vegetation that characterize the site.

The D.L. James House and its garden near Carmel is Charles Greene's individual masterpiece and his most unique landscape. Built on a rocky promontory

CELEBRATING REGIONAL RHYTHMS AND MATERIALS

Allow the cycles of the sun, the moon, and the stars to become celebrated events in your home and garden. In the house, consider adding windows or skylights that offer an easy view of daybreak or of the night sky. In the garden, design sitting or gathering places that naturally direct attention to the movements of sun and moon. Architectural elements such as terraces can be effective in providing such focus, as can sculptural objects and other garden artworks. Water gardens are among the most reflective garden features during day or night. A house and garden designed to celebrate celestial rhythms provides a rewarding connection with elemental forces in nature.

CELEBRATING REGIONAL RHYTHMS AND MATERIALS

Pay close attention to texture and translucency when working with plants and nonliving materials in the garden: they are important qualities that capture the nature of place. Translucent foliage will capture and redirect sunbeams in dramatic ways. Grasses are among the most luminous of garden plants, with fine, linear leaves that glow even in the low winter light. Sagebrushes (Artemisia spp.) are native to American deserts and California chaparral regions. Their silvery foliage is easily lit by sun or full moon, and they are fine choices for dry gardens. The varying surface textures of different stone types have a profound effect on the silhouettes and shadows they create.

Charles Greene's vast pool and imaginative
stonework at Green Gables, the Fleishhacker
family estate in Woodside, play beautifully
with the natural California light.

overlooking the Pacific Ocean, the house is in such beautiful harmony with the landscape that it is nearly impossible to distinguish between the two. Though there is a garden in the entry courtyard on the landward side, the essence of the gardens is the established native landscape of Monterey cypress (*Cupressus macrocarpa*) and pines.

BOK TOWER GARDENS:
A LYRICAL FLORIDA LANDSCAPE

A number of people involved with the Arts and Crafts Movement continued to live its ideals long after the movement's early popularity had waned. Like Charles Greene, their later contributions to the Arts and Crafts garden were sometimes great and wonderful.

Intimately involved with early-twentieth-century Arts and Crafts thinkers in the Philadelphia region, Edward Bok had been one of Will Price's early supporters in the initiation of the Rose Valley community. Price had also designed Bok's house in Upper Merion, Pennsylvania. Dutch emigrant Edward Bok made his fortune as the progressive editor of *The Ladies Home Journal,* and wished to follow his grandmother's advice to make the world "a bit better or more beautiful because you have lived in it." Completed in Lake Wales, Florida, in 1929, Bok Tower Gardens is the realization of Bok's dream.

Edward Bok was originally drawn to central Florida by the developing private community of Mountain Lake, designed by the Olmsted Brothers firm. While building a winter home at Mountain Lake, Bok fell in love with the natural beauty of a high point of land adjacent to the community. Known as Iron Mountain, this natural hill was the highest point in central Florida, 298 feet (91m) above sea level. Bok purchased the land and arranged for it to be developed as a garden devoted to the preservation and

Spanish moss (Tillandia usneoides) glows in afternoon sunlight streaming through live oaks at Bok Tower Gardens in Lake Wales, Florida.

appreciation of central Florida's flora and fauna, originally naming it Mountain Lake Sanctuary.

Frederick Law Olmsted, Jr., carried out the major design of the gardens, which featured an encompassing grove of native live oak (*Quercus virginiana*), that eventually grew to be naturally hung with Spanish moss. Olmsted also placed a reflecting pond at the gardens' center.

Set in a landscape of palms and live oak, the carillon tower is reflected in a central pool at Bok Tower Gardens.

Like William Morris, Gustav Stickley, and so many others involved with the Arts and Crafts Movement, Edward Bok believed in the good influence of the beautiful, and was interested in inviting a unity of the arts into everyday life. Recalling the glorious sound of carillons in his native Holland, Bok decided to build a great carillon tower at the sanctuary, and brought some of the country's best artists and craftsmen together make it a reality.

Built in Gothic style of native Florida coquina stone and Georgia marble, the tower rises 205 feet (62m) from its foundation at one end of the reflecting pond. The upper exterior is decorated with huge multicolored panels of Enfield tile, displaying stylized images of plants and animals in Edenic natural surroundings.

The main door of the tower was designed and crafted of brass by renowned metalworker Samuel Yellin, who had also done metalwork for Rose Valley. The door tells the story of Creation, with individual panels dedicated to various aspects of nature. The premier panel illustrates a great spreading tree, which ties the tower directly to the surrounding canopy of live oaks.

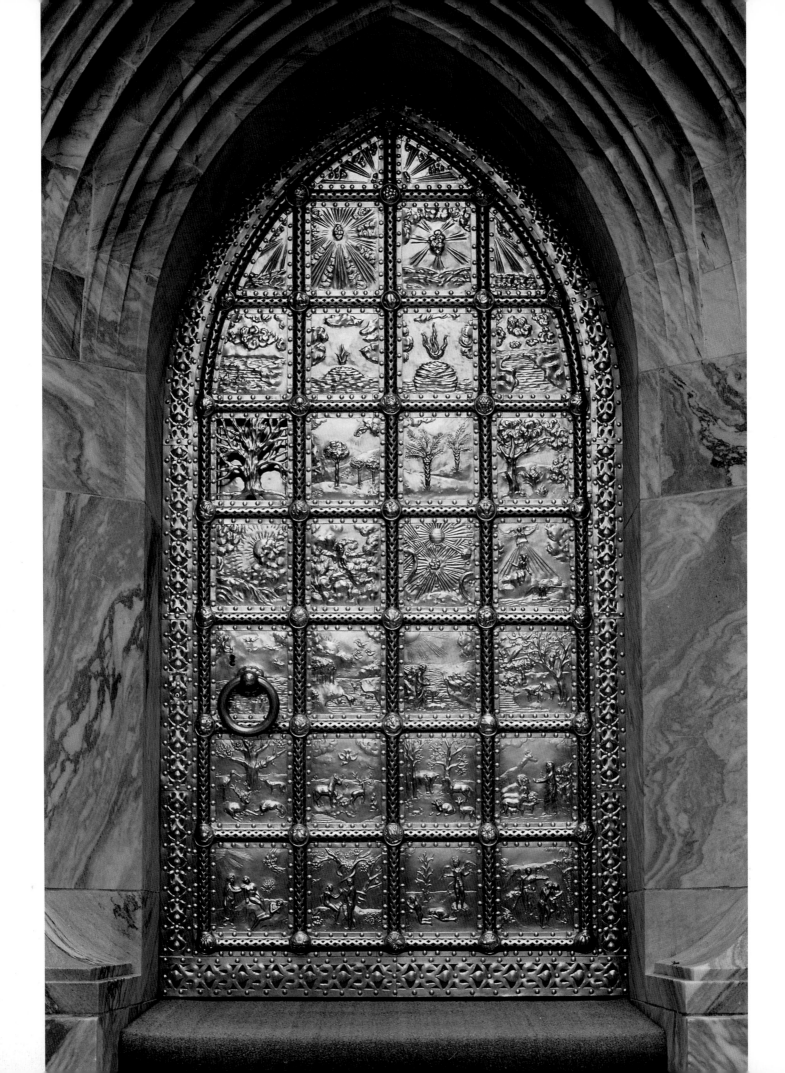

Entry to the carillon tower is through a
magnificent hammered brass door by
renowned metalworker Samuel Yellin. As the
door opens, sunlight floods the room and
illuminates a stunning Enfield tile mural
dedicated to the flora and fauna of Florida.

True to William Morris' traditions, the interior decoration of the tower is directly inspired by natural colors and forms, bringing a harmony to indoor and outdoor environments. The main floor consists of a breathtaking mural, also of Enfield tile, showing the spreading branches of the live oak, hung with Spanish moss. Within the branches, tile details depict animals native to

Florida. At the periphery, a waving ribbon symbolizes a transition to an aquatic realm, where individual images of fish and other water-loving animals appear. At the very center of the mural, a six-pointed star symbolizing life is overlaid on a stylized image of the native yellow lotus (*Nelumbo lutea*), which was revered by Florida's Seminole Indians.

Edward Bok's Florida sanctuary is a reminder that the garden is perhaps the perfect meeting place for the arts, and that a garden built with an inclusive vision is likely to remain a treasure for many generations.

FRANK LLOYD WRIGHT: UPDATING ARTS AND CRAFTS GARDEN IDEALS

Though Frank Lloyd Wright was an original member of the Chicago Arts and Crafts Society, founded in 1897, his long and extraordinarily productive career far outlasted the early high point of the Arts and Crafts Movement. Remaining active until his death in 1959, Wright continually sought to realize the Arts and Crafts ideals of simple, honest design, a reverence for place, and a unity of house and garden. For Wright, steeped in his family's Emersonian tradition, the garden *was* nature, and of those allied with the Arts and Crafts Movement in North America, Frank Lloyd Wright was among the most sensitive and accepting of the continent's diverse climate and landscape forms.

While the majority of English Arts and Crafts thinkers, and many American proponents as well, believed that the machine was inherently bad, Wright disagreed; he believed that it could, through appropriate application, help bring good design to greater numbers of people. He welcomed many simple advances in technology, such as the development of plate glass, and used them in his

OPPOSITE, TOP AND BOTTOM: *Frank Lloyd Wright's garden at Taliesin included old-fashioned favorites such as hollyhocks. He also considered his working farm an essential visual part of the designed landscape.*

architecture to effect a practical marriage with the elements of nature. Wright believed that "Buildings, too, are children of Earth and Sun," and outlined his philosophy in his 1954 book, *The Natural House*. In it he wrote, "it is by way of glass that the sunlit space as a reality becomes the most useful servant of a higher order of the human spirit...glass [will] make the garden be the building as much as the building will be the garden, the sky as treasured a feature of daily indoor life as the ground itself." A brief survey of Wright buildings in different regions illustrates how effective his designs were in achieving a harmony with nature.

Wright's own nature was Midwestern. He knew his native surroundings well, expressing his appreciation for them by stating "We of the Middle West are living on the prairie. The prairie has a beauty of its own and we should recognize and accentuate this natural beauty, its quiet level." Taliesin, his own

home near Spring Green, Wisconsin, is a fine example of the way Wright
fitted a building to its place. The lines of Taliesin are low and broad, reflecting
the breadth of the natural landscape. Wright was fond of old-fashioned
flowers such as hollyhocks, but he was equally welcoming of the plants of
forests and fields that comprised his "garden" in the larger sense. The farm
complex at Taliesin was more fitting a part of Wright's designed landscape

than any common flower border could ever be. Wright was ever intrigued with the bold forms of plants such as the American native staghorn sumac, abstracting it in architectural motifs and enjoying it in the wild garden.

Wright was at the center of a circle of architects and landscape architects known as the Prairie School. Though he never professed to be a landscape architect, Wright worked closely with pioneers including Jens Jensen (1860–1951), who did much to establish a tradition of gardening appropriate to the prairie region.

When Wright relocated to Arizona, building his Taliesin West complex outside Phoenix, he made no attempt to make it look like his familiar Wisconsin, but instead created both buildings and landscape as a tribute to the bold forms of the American desert. He later recalled, "I was struck by the beauty of the desert, by the clear sun-drenched air, by the stark geometry of

Wright recognized the architectural beauty of staghorn sumac, a common North American native species.

OPPOSITE: *A broad clump of staghorn sumac (Rhus typhina) grows at the B.H. Bradley House in Kenkakee, Illinois, which Wright designed in 1900.*

BELOW: *The same species of sumac glows with color in autumn.*

CELEBRATING REGIONAL RHYTHMS AND MATERIALS

Jens Jensen and Frank Lloyd Wright were familiar with stratified limestone from innumerable explorations through the midwestern landscape. The horizontal layering of this regional stone is distinct and recognizable, reflecting millions of years of accumulation of natural sediments. Jensen paid careful attention to preserving the horizontal nature of this stone when arranging it in his landscape designs.

The layering in natural rock outcrops may be horizontal, angled, or nearly vertical, but it is usually consistent within an individual outcrop. When creating naturalistic stonework in the garden, try to maintain a consistent orientation of the stone layers.

OPPOSITE: *Wright knew and sometimes worked with pioneering landscape architect Jens Jensen, who shared Wright's love of the native midwestern landscape. Jensen's plantings for Columbus Park, outside* *Chicaco, included native witch hazel (Hamamelis virginiana), which turns lemon yellow in autumn, and shadbush (Amelanchier canadensis), which acquires a distinctive salmon-colored glow in autumn.*

BELOW: *Jensen's design for Columbus Park featured a prairie river fed by water flowing over local stratified limestone.*

LEFT: *The Harold Price, Sr., House in Paradise Valley, Arizona, was designed by Wright and built in 1954. The house is quite open to the surrounding landscape, which is abundant with native desert species.*

BELOW: *Few landscapes surpass the natural color of the desert following winter rains. In March in Arizona, desert marigold (Baileya multiradiata), globe mallow (Sphaeralcea ambigua), and Coulter's lupine (Lupinus sparsiflorus) bloom together naturally.*

CELEBRATING REGIONAL RHYTHMS AND MATERIALS

Arid landscapes of the American Southwest were unfamiliar and disorienting to some gardeners during the Arts and Crafts period, and they saw little opportunity for beauty in these dry lands. Other designers, like Frank Lloyd Wright, embraced the bold forms, colors, and patterns of the desert, and celebrated them in the houses and gardens they made. Our modern understanding of the limited and precious nature of natural resources suggests that gardens that will thrive in local conditions are more important than ever before. William Morris' linking of beauty and utility continues to have significant meaning for modern landscape designers.

the mountains. The region was an inspiration in strong contrast to the lush, pastoral landscape of my native Wisconsin."

Like Charles Greene, Wright took delight in nuances of natural light in the landscape. At Taliesin West, he planned his canvas-roofed Garden Room to look out to the east, and described "the sun's early morning rays filling the room with sparkling light, the late afternoon sun hitting the canvas and illuminating the interior with a luscious golden light."

*Gossamer strands of ocotillo (*Fouquieria splendens*) contrast with saguaro cacti (*Carnegiea gigantea*) standing sentinel-like in the distance as the Arizona sun sets.*

A WINDOW ON NATURE

Frank Lloyd Wright continually looked for ways to provide occupants of a house with a sense of immersion in the garden and the surrounding native landscape. He firmly believed that well-designed architecture should provide a virtual window on nature. Wright's houses often included open terraces and large expanses of glass that provided a ready connection to the out-of-doors. In his day, Wright had only single-paned glass to work with, which was extremely inefficient in heated or air-conditioned houses. The broad array of double-paned, vacuum-insulated windows and doors available today offers efficient, nearly unlimited possibilities to coordinate indoor and outdoor views.

OPPOSITE, TOP AND BOTTOM:
Frank Lloyd Wright designed Kentuck Knob in 1953 for the I. N. Hagen family of Uniontown, Pennsylvania. Generous windows and a perimeter terrace offer constant views of the surrounding garden and native woodlands.

Wright was a consistent advocate for preserving the essential nature of a site, understanding that architecture "accentuates the character of the landscape if the architecture is right." His design for Fallingwater, near Mill Run, Pennsylvania, provides for an intimate experience with its famous waterfall. With its open winter views and enveloping summer leafiness, the house is equally eloquent in telling the story of the surrounding deciduous forest Wright rarely focused on formal gardens, but rather let native plantings come up to the edge of his buildings when practical.

The naturalness of Wright's designs was easily adapted to modest scale, which is evident in his later "Usonian" (a term coined by Wright from the words "U.S. own home") houses, including Kentuck Knob in Pennsylvania and the Seth Petersen Cottage in Wisconsin. Wright was intent on incorporating into modest, affordable houses all the best of his design innovations.

Wright never relinquished the notion that through imagination and appropriate use of technology the house and garden could be as one. Combining this ideal with his unbiased embrace of regional landscapes, Wright's work frequently stands as the most persuasive achievement of a harmony with nature.

Wright's architecture so subtly meets the earth that it is difficult to tell where the house begins and where nature leaves off. To this day, local natives such as rhododendron (Rhododendron maximum), at left, and sweet birch (Betula lenta), below, grow up to the very foundations of Fallingwater, opposite.

LEFT: *Measuring less than 900 square feet (83.7 sq m) in area, the Seth Peterson cottage still manages to offer native stone floors and walls, a great hearth to gather around, and a panoramic view through the immediate woodlands down to adjacent Mirror Lake. Designed in 1958, the cottage was one of Wright's last designs. It survives as proof that inspired design can be distilled into the most modest of spaces.*

KEEPING NATURE
CLOSE TO HEART AND HAND

T here are many others artists and designers, even after Wright, who adopted Arts and Crafts principles and combined them with their own personal artistry to live their lives in true harmony with nature. Wharton Esherick (1887–1970) is a model among them.

Starting out as a painter of landscapes, Esherick eventually found his ideal medium for artistic expression in wood sculpture, using primarily eastern hardwoods. Esherick hand-built his stone home and studio, set in an informal woodland garden in the hills near Paoli, Pennsylvania.

Wharton Esherick's home and studio is loosely modeled after a Pennsylvania barn and silo. The color palette in the stucco is drawn from local autumn hues.

Though many of Esherick's works were highly abstract, his inspiration came largely from his own observations. Esherick positioned his bed on a level with the windowsill in his second-floor bedroom, so that he would wake each day to events in the surrounding landscape. One of Esherick's masterpieces, his own drop-leaf desk made in 1927 of red oak, expresses Esherick's insight into the nature of the deciduous forest. The low carving on the center panel abstracts a broad view into the woodland winter canopy. The panels below are decorated with abstracts of various branching patterns of woodland trees. Fittingly, the top panels show birds gliding silently above the roof of the forest.

LIVING THE IDEAL

Perhaps the most essential lesson of the Arts and Crafts Movement is that, when broadly defined, the garden is the ideal meeting place for a balance of art and science, of handcraft and machine technology. Our continuing search for a healthy, harmonious existence will always require new input and insight. For example, the naturalism introduced by William Robinson's early notions of wild gardening has become a widely accepted convention, but since then the science of ecology has raised our awareness of the complexity of nature. Robinson failed to distinguish between "wild" and "native" plants, using the words interchangeably. His idea of naturalizing hardy bulbs in temperate forests has proved relatively innocuous; however, Robinson did not anticipate the negative effects of introduced exotic plants that "naturalize" too well, displacing the existing flora.

Beauty is a powerful motivating force, and it seems certain that artistic insight will play a major role in defining tomorrow's gardens. It may also help us understand the complex nature of our time. Supporting much of the artistry and style of the Arts and Crafts Movement was a deep belief in the power of firsthand observation. The colors and patterns associated with the

OPPOSITE TOP: *Esherick awoke daily to a contemplation of nature.*

OPPOSITE BOTTOM: *The carved panels of Esherick's own red oak desk abstract living forms and patterns from the native forest.*

ABOVE AND OPPOSITE: *Spring bulbs including blue* Scilla *and* Chionodoxa *and golden winter aconite (*Eranthus hyemalis*) are naturalized below native forest trees at Winterthur Museum, Garden, and Library in Delaware. Winterthur represents the greatest North American expression of William Robinson's vision of the Wild Garden.*

period owe much to an awakened interest in ordinary natural materials and events. Thoughtful observers found considerable enlightenment in the process.

The very nature of the garden is such that it encourages observation, invites contemplation. At its best, the garden is a celebration of human community, of place, and of the interrelationship of all living things. It is one of the simplest paths to daily satisfaction, and one of the steadiest for achieving a true harmony with nature.

Resources

ART AND ARTIFACTS

THE ARTS & CLAY COMPANY
24 Pikes Lane
Woodstock, NY 12498
(914) 679-6875

ARTS & CRAFTS PERIOD
 TEXTILES
5427 Telegraph Avenue #W2
Oakland, CA 94609
(510) 654-1645

AURORA STUDIOS
(Michael Adams metalwork)
www.dreamscape.com/aurorastudios

BRADBURY & BRADBURY ART
 WALLPAPER
P.O. Box 155-Y3
Benicia, CA 94510
(707) 746-1900
www.bradbury.com

CRAFTSMAN AUCTIONS
1485 West Housatonic
Pittsfield, MA 01201
(800) 448-7828

CRAFTSMEN HARDWARE CO.
P.O. Box 161
Marceline, MO 64658
(660) 376-2481
www.craftsmenhardware.com

CROWN CITY HARDWARE
1047 N. Allen Avenue
Pasadena, CA 91104-3298
Catalog Direct: (626) 794-0234
Orders Only: (800) 950-1047
www.crowncityhardware.com

EPHRAIM FAIENCE ART POTTERY
P.O. Box 168
Deerfield, WI 53531
(888) 704-POTS or (608)-764-1302

FULPER TILE
P.O. Box 373
Yardley, PA 19067
(215) 736-8512

EVERGREEN STUDIOS
(V. Michael Ashford metalwork)
6543 Alpine Drive SW
Olympia, WA 98512
(360) 352-0694
www.evergreenstudios.com

JAX ARTS & CRAFTS RUGS
109 Parkway
Berea, KY 40403
(606) 986-5410
www.4berea.com/jaxco

THE MISSION OAK SHOP
109 Main St.
Putnam, CT 06260
(800) 448-7828
www.artsncrafts.com

MORAVIAN POTTERY
 & TILEWORKS
130 Swamp Road
Doylestown, PA 18901
(215) 345-6722

MOTAWI TILEWORKS
33 North Staebler, Suite 2
Ann Arbor, MI 48103
(734) 213-0017
www.motawi.com

THE PERSIAN CARPET
5634 Chapel Hill Boulevard
Durham, NC 27707
(800) 333-1801

PEWABIC POTTERY
10125 E. Jefferson Ave.
Detroit, MI 48214
(313) 822-0954
Fax (313)822-6266
www.pewabic.com

DAVID RAGO AUCTIONS INC.
333 North Main Street
Lambertville, NJ 08530
(609) 397-9374
www.ragoarts.com

SENECA TILES INC.
7100 South County Road 23
Attica, OH 44807
(800) 426-4335
www.senecatiles.com

SIEBERT & RICE
(TERRA-COTTA POTS)
P.O. Box 365
Short Hills, NJ 07078
(973) 467-8266
www.seibert-rice.com

TREADWAY GALLERY INC.
2029 Madison Road
Cincinnati, OH 45208
(513) 321-6742
www.treadwaygallery.com

SAMUEL YELLIN
METALWORKERS CO.
721 Moore Avenue
Bryn Mawr, PA 19010-2208
(610) 527-2334
Fax (610) 527-2412

SOCIETIES AND FOUNDATIONS

THE ARTS & CRAFTS SOCIETY
1194 Bandera Drive
Ann Arbor, MI 48103
(734) 665-4729
www.arts-crafts.com

BERKELEY ARCHITECTURAL
HERITAGE ASSOCIATION
P.O. Box 1137
Berkeley, California 94701
(510) 845-1632

THE FRANK LLOYD WRIGHT
FOUNDATION
Taliesin West
P.O. Box 4430
Scottsdale, AZ 85261-4430
www.franklloydwright.org

THE FRANK LLOYD WRIGHT
BUILDING CONSERVANCY
4657-B North Ravenswood Avenue
Chicago, IL 60604-4509
(773) 784-7334
www.swcp.com/flw

TILE HERITAGE FOUNDATION
P.O. Box 1850
Healdsburg, CA 95448
(707) 431-8453
www.tileheritage.org

WILLIAM MORRIS SOCIETY
OF CANADA
53 Berkeley Court
Unionville
Ontario L3R 6L9
(905) 475-9370
www.yorku.ca/faculty/mckenna/wmsc

REFERENCES AND READINGS

Books

A *History of Rose Valley*, edited by Peter Ham, Eleanore Price Mather, Judy Walton, and Patricia Ward

A *Poor Sort of Heaven, A Good Sort of Earth: The Rose Valley Arts & Crafts Experiment*, edited by William Ayres and Ann Barton Brown

America's Taj Mahal: The Singing Tower of Florida by Edward W. Bok

American Art Pottery by David Rago

American Art Pottery by Vance Koehler

American Art Tile: 1876–1941 by Norman Karlson

The American Bungalow by Clay Lancaster

American Arts & Crafts: Virtue in Design by Leslie Greene Bowman

American Bungalow Style by Robert Winter and Alexander Vertikoff

American Masterworks: The Twentieth Century House by Kenneth Frampton and David Larkin

An American Architecture by Frank Lloyd Wright

Archibald Knox, edited by Stephen A. Martin

The Architect and the American Country House by Mark Alan Hewitt

The Architecture of Frank Lloyd Wright: A Complete Catalog by William Allin Storrer

Arts & Crafts Architecture by Peter Davey

Arts & Crafts Carpets by Malcolm Haslam

Arts & Crafts Design in America: A State by State Guide by James Massey and Shirley Maxwell

Arts & Crafts Gardens by Wendy Hitchmough

Arts & Crafts Gardens by Gertrude Jekyll and Lawrence Weaver

The Arts & Crafts Movement by Elizabeth Cumming and Wendy Kaplan

The Arts & Crafts Movement: A Study of Its Sources, Ideals and Influence on Design Theory by Gillian Naylor

The Arts & Crafts Movement in the Cotswolds by Mary Greensted

The Arts & Crafts Movement in California: Living the Good Life by Kenneth R. Trapp and others

The Arts & Crafts Studio of Dirk Van Erp by Dorothy Lamoureaux

Arts & Crafts Style and Spirit by Chase Reynolds Ewald

Batchelder Tilemaker by Robert W. Winter

Built for the Ages: A History of the Grove Park Inn by Bruce E. Johnson

California Bungalow by Robert Winter

California Design 1910, edited by Timothy Andersen, Eudorah Moore, and Robert Winter

California Gardens: Creating a New Eden by David C. Streatfield

California Impressionism by William H. Gerdts and Will South

C.F.A. Voysey by Wendy Hitchmough

Charles Rennie Mackintosh by Fiona and Isla Hackney

The Color Encyclopedia of Ornamental Grasses by Rick Darke

Craftsman Fabric and Needlework by Gustav Stickley

Craftsman-Style Houses by the editors of Fine Homebuilding

The Designs of Archibald Knox for Liberty & Co. by A.J. Tilbrook

Details of Frank Lloyd Wright: The California Work, 1909–1974 by Judith Dunham

The Edwardian Garden by David Ottewill

El Alisal: Where History Lingers by Jane Apostol

The Face of North America: The Natural History of a Continent by Peter Farb

Fallingwater: A Frank Lloyd Wright Country House by Edgar Kaufmann, Jr.

Fay Jones by Robert Adams Ivy, Jr.

Frank Lloyd Wright: A Biography by Meryle Secrest

Frank Lloyd Wright: Architecture and Nature by Donald Hoffmann

Frank Lloyd Wright in Michigan by A. Dale Northup

Frank Lloyd Wright in Wisconsin by Kristin Visser

Frank Lloyd Wright Selected Houses #7 by Bruce Brooks Pfeiffer

Frank Lloyd Wright: The Masterworks by Bruce Brooks Pfeiffer and David Larkin

Frank Lloyd Wright's Fallingwater: The House and Its History by Donald Hoffmann

Frederick Law Olmsted : Designing the American Landscape by Charles E. Beveridge

Gardens of a Golden Afternoon: The Story of a Partnership: Edwin Lutyens and Gertrude Jekyll by Jane Brown

The Gardens of William Morris by Jill Duchess of Hamilton, Penny Hart, and John Simons

Gertrude Jekyll at Munstead Wood: Writing, Horticulture, Photography, Homebuilding by Judith Tankard and Martin Wood

Gimson and the Barnsleys by Mary Greensted

Grandmother's Garden: The Old-Fashioned American Garden 1865–1915 by May Brawley Hill

Greene & Greene: Architecture as Fine Art by Randell L. Makinson

Greene & Greene: Masterworks by Bruce Smith

Greene & Greene: The Passion and the Legacy by Randell L. Makinson

Gustave Baumann: Nearer to Art by Martin Krause, Madeline Carol Yurtseven, and David Acton

Gustav Stickley: The Craftsman by Mary Ann Smith

Hand of a Craftsman : The Woodcut Technique of Gustave Baumann by David Acton

Gustav Stickley: The Craftsman by Mary Ann Smith

Hand of a Craftsman : The Woodcut Technique of Gustave Baumann by David Acton

Handmade Tiles: Designing, Making, Decorating by Frank Giorgini

Henry Chapman Mercer and the Moravian Pottery and Tileworks by Cleota Reed

Houses & Gardens by E.L. Lutyens by Lawrence Weaver

The Ideal Home 1900–1920: The History of Twentieth-Century American Craft edited by Janet Kardon

In the Arts & Crafts Style by Barbara Mayer

In the Nature of Materials: The Buildings of Frank Lloyd Wright—1887–1941 by Henry-Russell Hitchcock

Jens Jensen: Maker of Natural Parks and Gardens by Robert E. Grese

The Life of Sir Edwin Lutyens by Christopher Hussey

Edwin Lutyens by Mary Lutyens

Lutyens and the Edwardians: An English Architect and His Clients by Jane Brown

Many Masks: A Life of Frank Lloyd Wright by Brendan Gill

Mohonk: Its People and Spirit by Larry E. Burgess

Native Gardens for Dry Climates by Sally Wasowski with Andy Wasowski

The Native Plant Primer by Carole Ottesen

The Natural Habitat Garden by Ken Druse

The Natural House by Frank Lloyd Wright

Nature by Ralph Waldo Emerson

Nature and Ideology: Natural Garden Design in the Twentieth Century edited by Joachim Wolschke-Bulmahn

O California!: Nineteenth and Early Twentieth Century California Landscapes and Observations edited by Stephen Vincent

Philadelphia's Progressive Orphanage: The Carson Valley School by David R. Contosta

The Prairie School: Frank Lloyd Wright and His Midwest Contemporaries by H. Allen Brooks

Prairie in the City: Naturalism in Chicago's Parks, 1870–1940 by the Chicago Historical Society

Reflecting Nature: Garden Designs from Wild Landscapes by Jerome Malitz and Seth Malitz

Regional Garden Design in the United States, edited by Therese O'Malley and Marc Treib

Second Nature: Four Early San Diego Landscape Painters by Martin E. Petersen

Southern California Gardens: An Illustrated History by Victoria Padilla

Taliesin West: In the Realm of Ideas edited by Suzette A. Lucas

Toward a Simpler Way of Life: The Arts & Crafts Architects of California by Robert Winter

Wall & Water Gardens by Gertrude Jekyll

The Wild Garden by William Robinson

The Winterthur Garden: Henry Francis du Pont's Romance with the Land by Denise Magnani and others.

The Wright Style: Recreating the Spirit of Frank Lloyd Wright by Carla Lind

CD-ROM

The Arts & Crafts Devolution (Gustav Stickley's *The Craftsman* on CD-ROM)
InterAlios Communications
P.O. Box 41540
Pasadena, CA 91104
(626) 432-6677
www.interalioscom.com

The Craftsman on CD-ROM
Interactive Bureau
251 Park Avenue South, 10th Floor
New York, NY 10010
(212) 292-1900
Fax (212)-292-1914

Periodicals

American Bungalow Magazine/American Bungalow News
P.O. Box 756123
S. Baldwin Avenue
Sierra Madre, CA 91025-0756
(800) 350-3363
www.ambungalow.com

Style 1900: The Quarterly Journal of the Arts & Crafts Movement
333 North Main Street
Lambertville, NJ 08530
(609) 397-4104
www.ragoarts.com

Frank Lloyd Wright Quarterly
Taliesin West
  P.O. Box 4430
Scottsdale, Arizona 85261-4430

PLACES TO VISIT

THE AHWAHNEE (INN)
Yosemite National Park
California, 95389
(209) 372-1463

BOK TOWER GARDENS
1151 Tower Boulevard
Lake Wales, FL 33853-3412
(863) 676-1408
www.boktower.org

CRAFTSMAN FARMS
2352 Rt. 10-West
Box 5
Morris Plains, NJ 07950
(973) 540-1165
Fax: (973) 540-1167
www.parsippany.net/craftsmanfarms

THE WHARTON ESHERICK
  MUSEUM
P.O. Box 595
Paoli, PA 19301
(610) 644-5822
www.levins.com/esherick

EL ALISAL (CHARLES LUMMIS
  HOUSE)
200 East Avenue 43
Los Angeles, CA 90031
(213) 222-0546

FALLINGWATER
P.O. Box R
Mill Run, PA 15464
(724) 329-8501
www.paconserve.org

FONTHILL (HENRY CHAPMAN
  MERCER HOME)
East Court Street and Swamp Road
Doylestown, PA 18901
(215) 348-9461

THE FRANK LLOYD WRIGHT
  HOME & STUDIO
951 Chicago Avenue
Oak Park, IL 60302
(708) 848-1976
www.wrightplus.org

THE GAMBLE HOUSE
4 Westmoreland Place
Pasadena, CA 91103
(626) 793-3334
www.gamblehouse.usc.edu

THE GROVE PARK INN
290 Macon Avenue
Asheville, NC 28804
(800) 438-5800
www.groveparkinn.com

GRAVETYE MANOR NEAR EAST
　GRINSTEAD
West Sussex RH19 4LJ
　England
Tel.: (44) 01342 810567
Fax: (44) 01342 810080
www.relaischateaux.fr/gravetye

HEDGEROW THEATER
64 Rose Valley Road
Rose Valley, PA 19086
(610) 565-4211

HESTERCOMBE
Cheddon Fitzpain, Taunton
Somerset, England
Tel. (44) 01823 337222

KENTUCK KNOB
P.O. Box 305
Chalk Hill, PA 15421-0305
(724) 329-1901
Fax (724) 329-0977

LITTLE THAKEHAM
Merrywood Lane
Storrington, West Sussex RH20 3HE
　England
Telephone (44) 01903 744416
Fax (44) 01903 745022

MOHONK MOUNTAIN HOUSE
New Paltz, NY 12561
(800) 772-6646
www.mohonk.com

MORAVIAN POTTERY
　& TILEWORKS
130 Swamp Road
Doylestown, PA 18901
(215) 345-6722

THE MORRIS ARBORETUM
9414 Meadowbrook Avenue
Philadelphia, PA 19118
(215) 247-5777
www.upenn.edu/morris

SETH PETERSEN COTTAGE
Reservations c/o Sand County Service
　Company
Box 409
Lake Delton, WI 53940
(608) 254-6551

TALIESIN
Spring Green, Wisconsin
Tour reservations (608) 588-7900

TALIESIN WEST
Scottsdale, Arizona
Recorded Tour Information
　(602) 860-8810 Reservations:
　(602) 860-2700 ext. 494/495

WILLOWWOOD ARBORETUM
Longview Road
Chester, NJ
(908) 234-0992

WINTERTHUR MUSEUM,
　GARDEN, AND LIBRARY
Winterthur, DE 19735
(800) 448-3883
www.winterthur.org

ONLINE EVENTS LISTINGS

AMERICAN BUNGALOW
　NEWS & EVENTS
www.ambungalow.com/abmag/calend1

THE ARTS & CRAFTS SOCIETY
　EVENTS CALENDAR
www.arts-crafts.com/events/events

ONLINE SITES

BROADACRE: THE ALL-WRIGHT
　SITE
www.geocities.com/SoHo/1469/flw

FRANK LLOYD WRIGHT IN
　WISCONSIN
www.wrightinwisconsin.org
The William Morris Home Page
www.ccny.cuny.edu/wmorris/morris

Index